THE HOME-SCHOOL CONNECTION

THE HOME-SCHOOL CONNECTION

GUIDELINES FOR WORKING WITH PARENTS

JACQUELINE McGILP and MAUREEN MICHAEL

Heinemann
Portsmouth, NH

STAFFORD LIBRARY
COLUMBIA COLLEGE
1001 ROGERS STREET
COLUMBIA, MO 65216

Heinemann
A Division of Reed Publishing (USA) Inc.
361 Hanover Street Portsmouth, NH 03801-3912
Offices and agents throughout the world

Copyright © 1994 Jacqueline McGilp and Maureen Michael

All rights reserved.
No part of this book may be reproduced in any other form
or by any electronic or mechanical means, including
information storage and retrieval systems, without permission in writing from the
publisher, except by a reviewer, who may quote brief passages in a review.

ISBN 0 435 08820 3.

Published simultaneously in the United States
by Heinemann and in Australia by
Eleanor Curtain Publishing
906 Malvern Road
Armadale, Australia 3143

Production by Sylvana Scannapiego, Island Graphics
Edited by Marion Russell
Design by David Constable
Cover photographs by Sara Curtain
Printed in Australia by Impact Printing Pty Ltd

Contents

Part 1
Understanding the Connection

1	Parents and Schools	1
	Kinds of Parent Involvement	2
	Educational Roles	2
	The Home-School Learning Connection	3
	The Pennycoe Project	4
2	All Parents are Teachers	5
	How Parents Teach	5
	Parents are Proud Teachers	7
3	Education for Living	8
	Who Does What?	10
4	The Pennycoe Project	13
	Structure	15
	Monitoring the Project	16
	The Outcomes	17
5	Educational Roles for Parents in Schools	20
	Spectators	20
	Organisers	21
	Instructors	21
	Learners	23
	More than one role	23
6	Home and Community Settings	25
	The Hobsons Run an Evening Class	26
	Mr Hearne Takes a Year 4 Class	30
	Parents Organise an Art Excursion	31

Part 2
Making the Connection

7	Creating the Climate	39
	A Climate of Confidence	39
	Management	43
8	Training Sessions	44
	Who's Responsible for Training?	45
	Who Does the Training?	46
	Training Modes	46
	Timing of Sessions	47

9 Discussion Program for the School Community	49
The Program	50
Introductory Session	52
Subsequent Sessions	55
Discussion Program for Teachers	55
10 Curriculum Plan	58
Appendix: Blackline Masters	60
References	83
Index	85

PART 1
Understanding the Connection

1
Parents and Schools

As professionals, teachers have a responsibility for children's learning, but this responsibility is shared with parents. Especially since the 1970s, when professional status was challenged in many spheres, the teaching profession faced questions such as: Should those with credentials reserve the right to define valued knowledge and to deliver educational services to the community? (Bernstein 1981; Pettit 1980) Shouldn't families have a role in the formal education of their children?

In a parallel development, responsibility for socialisation, once perceived as the prerogative of the home, is now perceived more broadly as social learning not only during childhood but throughout the life cycle and in a variety of organisational contexts. Our purposes for schooling and education have extended to *education for living*.

Associated changes in the educational policies of governments have increased community control of education. Many recent policy statements name community members, including parents, in significant positions, for example, as members of school boards and as evaluators, with the right and responsibility to take an active interest in their children's progress.

Today, parents want effective involvement in the formulation of educational policy; and the importance of parental involvement is acknowledged in the vision and mission statements of schools and in school charters.

Kinds of Parent Involvement

Parents can be involved in a variety of ways with the school: as *audience, spectators, fund raisers, aides, organisers, instructors, learners, policy makers, decision makers* and *advocates* of school happenings (Gordon 1970; Schikedanz 1977; McGilp 1991, 1992, 1993; Braggett 1980; Davies 1986).

Many of these roles have been familiar for a long time. As *audience*, parents read school notice sheets and attend open days, school concerts, parent nights and sports functions. As *fund raisers* they have run many a raffle and a fete. They are *organisers* of social events, tuckshops and working bees. They are staunch advocates of, say, nutritional lunches or school uniforms.

More recently developed roles are also familiar: *decision maker* on a school planning committee, *policy maker* on the school or regional education board.

In each of these roles, parents make important connections with their children's school and support its activities in valued ways.

Educational Roles

This book is concerned, however, with less familiar, *educational* roles in which schools use – and develop – parents' competence to enrich the actual school program. It shows how to establish and maintain a home-school connection in which parents:

- Visit classrooms
- Observe how various teaching and learning methods affect the efforts of their children
- Organise classroom materials, and
- Actually instruct the children.

The key *educational* roles are *spectators, organisers, instructors* and *learners*.

SPECTATORS

Parents attend lessons or other sessions conducted in the school, homes or the community in order to observe and encourage children's learning.

PARENT ROLES IN SCHOOLS

Audience
Spectators
Fund raisers
Aides
Organisers
Instructors
Learners
Policy makers
Decision makers
Advocates

Figure 1
Parent roles in schools
Blackline master in Appendix

ORGANISERS
Parents assist teachers and children but do not teach. They prepare materials, design worksheets and gather other aids in readiness for the lessons whether at school, in the home or in the community. They also organise the involvement of other parents.

INSTRUCTORS
Researchers find it useful to distinguish between three kinds of instructors: the *experts* who are usually professionally qualified and practising the knowledge and skills in which they instruct the children – and who are fluent in its discourse; the *competent* instructors whose competence usually arises from their interests and hobbies – and who often have well developed skills in step-by-step instruction; and the *skilled if trained* instructors who attend training sessions at the school to learn skills which they subsequently teach to the children – and who usually rely on written lesson plans for guiding the children's efforts.

LEARNERS
Parents acquire skills by attending training sessions arranged by the school. The purpose of such learning can include becoming a *skilled if trained* instructor of children (see above).

The Home-School Learning Connection

Many studies have demonstrated the effectiveness of parents as supervisors, tutors and good models of learning in school settings. Of particular interest have been projects with disadvantaged communities in which parents, despite their disadvantage, were able to help their children to improve in mathematics, reading and languages (McConnell 1976, 1979).

This book shows how to forge a *learning* connection between home and school, one in which home and school work together, listen to each other and make good use of the variety of learning experiences available in the school, the home and the community.

In this kind of home-school connection, parents contribute their expertise and interests to provide the curriculum with a richness and variety that nurtures children's learning. This kind of home-school connection not only benefits the academic achievement of children but also creates a new and lively working relationship between home and school (Gordon 1970:13-14).

The means of involvement depends on the school's vision, belief in, and acknowledgement of, the parents' competence; and the school's encouragement of parents to adopt various roles. Considerable experience and practical support is needed, however, to have the home-school connection in good shape.

THE HOME-SCHOOL CONNECTION

The Pennycoe Project

Many of the strategies, procedures, case stories and examples cited in this book are drawn from the experience at 'Pennycoe', a school that successfully pursues the home-school connection. The 500 children at 'Pennycoe' are aged between 5 and 12 years and are organised in classes at seven year levels. One of the authors conducted a research study of Pennycoe's home-school connection program for a Year 4 class. Chapter 4 describes the operation of the Pennycoe Project.

2
All Parents are Teachers

Parents teach their children from the time they are babies and, for as long as children remain in their care, continue to teach them what they consider to be important. Encouraging a smile, the first chuckles, responses and first steps, are all aspects of parents' helping children to learn. Parents teach children to develop personal hygiene habits such as washing their hands and cleaning their teeth; to practise safety rules for crossing roads; and to value being friendly, polite and accepting of others.

Schools expect parents to teach children certain skills prior to school – mastery of buttons and zips, tying of shoe laces, recognition of their names and of colours and common objects around the home. Parents see it as their task to teach their children these and other skills. Parents guide their children's progress thus building children's self-esteem.

Parents expect schools to continue developing children as social beings who are accepted in, and contribute to, society because of the persons they are and the gifts and talents they share. Parents, in turn, reinforce school learning.

How Parents Teach
Parents teach their children by answering their questions about themselves, their families, friends and other people, how things are done, nature, society and the world itself. Parents teach by

THE HOME-SCHOOL CONNECTION

encouragement, demonstration, modelling, revising and monitoring children's efforts. They often use step-by-step instruction to enable children to be successful in their efforts. In teaching children to set the table, for instance, parents encourage children to help them. They teach children to recognise the knives, forks and spoons. They demonstrate the conventional positions for placing particular items of cutlery; and revise the process over and over again. They encourage the children to complete the task bit by bit and support their efforts as they do so. And when parents know that their children have acquired a skill or capacity, they encourage them to use it freely and independently. Parents know how to build on what children know, show them other ways, correct and praise children's efforts, and give them further opportunities for practice.

Once children are at school, parents and teachers perform complementary roles in teaching children everyday skills, social skills, self-care and problem solving; and in stimulating intellectual and academic attitudes and habits. The setting of homework implies that children study at home. Parents are expected to:
- Supervise children's learning
- Encourage study habits
- Reinforce certain skills

- Set standards
- Praise children's efforts.

Homework requires parent co-operation, understanding and a common standard of expectations by the home and the school.

Parents are Proud Teachers

It is a wonderful experience to listen to parents talking together. The conversation usually includes comments about their children – how they are growing, what they like, what they do and what they learn. Parents recognise their teaching ability:

'I taught her to say *Dad*.'

'He learnt chess from me.'

'We teach our children a lot about nature. It is easy when you live in the bush.'

Parents also supervise music practice and coach the sports team. Parents teach their children what they want them to learn – be it personal hygiene, safety rules, respect for others or certain games. Parents teach their children what they value. Parents are proud of their teaching efforts!

It is important that teachers listen to parents telling how they teach their children to look after themselves, how they arrange pre-school activities, and how they choose stimulating intellectual activities and learning opportunities for their children. Schools can build on parents' methods of teaching in establishing a strong, two-way, home-school connection to assist children's learning.

3
Education for Living

Each child is unique with personality, gifts and talents to be developed. Learning takes place not only at school but at home, in the wider community and everywhere that a child is. Learning can take place while children chat at home. Learning can take place in the busy local supermarket or by the tranquil river. Schools look to the total development of students and acknowledge the need to care for children and teach them skills for living their lives well.

This view of *education for living* is reinforced through a home-school connection that relates school learning, family living and community experience. Parents and teachers reinforce the importance of gaining knowledge and skills for living well. School activities are therefore integrated with the other daily life experiences of children. Somecontexts for *educating for living* are suggestedbelow.

At the supermarket

Children can learn the value of money, decision making and budgeting. They can gain an understanding of the effort it takes to meet family needs.

8

Education for Living

In the local factory
Children might observe how the work of these individuals and groups helps us all. They learn about dependence and interdependence.

> The Clothes Factory.
> I went to the Clothing Factory. I saw the denim material for making jeans. A man cut out the jeans. and four women sewed them up. They worked quickly at the factory. I wouldn't be able to get my jeans if they weren't sent to the Shop. Thank-you factory workers for my jeans.

At the retirement hostel
Children hear stories from elderly people about their lives. They gain insights into living in the past, its hardships and rewards. They learn from the advice and wisdom of others' experience.

In sports teams
Children learn co-operative skills and team work. They can learn that participation and playing fairly are more important than winning.

The school excursion
In the case of the art excursion, described in this chapter, children became conscious of the beauty of their local gully; experienced the value of novel roles and relationships with parents as formal instructors, supervisors and organisers; and learnt some specialist skills that are not normally part of a school curriculum.

THE HOME-SCHOOL CONNECTION

The Art Excursion

During autumn, on a Saturday afternoon, a painting excursion was arranged for Year 4 students at the local scenic gully. Parents and teachers had arranged the date, considered alternative venues and made the necessary arrangements for paints, brushes, water, rags, paper, pastels and easels to be taken to the scene. Transport was arranged for the children, parents and teachers.

In discussion, parents and teachers had decided the roles and activities. Some parents organised the materials while other parents taught the children. The children were to:
- Use water colours to paint a chosen spot in the gully
- Use pastels to draw a hidden creature amid the pebbles
- Use oils to paint a small plant
- Write about the experience in the gully

This experience of the beauty of the local environment was made possible through the co-operation of the home and school. The excursion was part of one school's home-school connection program.

Who Does What?

In *educating for living*, each child's learning is seen as influenced by the home, school and community. At different times these three groups individually, and as partners, contribute to children's progress. Schools, homes and communities are each initiators, instructors, facilitators and encouragers of *education for living*, as illustrated below.

As initiators
- Schools establish a home-school connection program
- Parents suggest that children learn hobbies
- Communities organise events such as art exhibitions.

As instructors and facilitators
- Schools teach children swimming and mouth-to-mouth resuscitation
- Parents demonstrate how to cook, garden and catch fish
- Communities provide learn-to-swim campaigns or Life Be In It sessions.

As encouragers
- Schools encourage children to participate in community sport
- Parents listen to their children reading
- Communities provide schemes and awards such as Young Achievers Award, photography, science and mathematics competitions.

In education for living, the home, school and community work together consciously, explicitly and by design, to develop children's capacities.

THE HOME-SCHOOL CONNECTION

4
The Pennycoe Project

Pennycoe has about five hundred students aged between 5 and 12 years and organised in classes at seven year levels. Even before the home-school connection project, it welcomed questions from parents, their visits on open days and sports days, and their sharing in the social events – annual barbecues, dinner dances and art shows. When surveyed just before the project was commenced, a high proportion of parents was satisfied with the school, the curriculum and the care of their children; they neither complained about nor challenged school happenings.

Education for living was valued at Pennycoe. The school systematically invited visitors and engaged professionals to provide the children with a variety of learning experiences and perspectives which were integrated into the school program. A community excursion was a regular part of the school program for every class. Observers of the sessions taken by expert visitors recorded incidental comments of the children, such as:

'My dad is an artist.'
'Mum teaches dancing.'
'We have an art gallery.'
'I wrote sports reports with Dad.'

Parents' occupations and interests, according to students, covered a wide range of experience. Teachers learnt much about the richness of parents' lives. Was there any reason why parents could not add to students' learning? Could more parents become interested in working with the children in the school program?

The principal and three of the staff members, advocates of the home-school *learning* connection, invited parent involvement in the teaching of *the arts* at the Year 4 level, stating their belief in the value of every opportunity for showing children that school learning has relevance in the home and in the community.

Pennycoe decided to commence its home-school connection with a year-long, arts-based project for its Year 4 children. At the time of the project, the school community had decided on the arts curriculum as the one most in need of renewal; and the school was already paying for the expertise of professional artists, poets, musicians, dancers and dramatists in the community.

Pennycoe planned to continue using the arts professionals but to have their sessions observed by parents with similar expertise or competence. This first set of parents would then conduct other sessions with the children and would also train a second set of parents to be able to participate in similar activities, frequently through having them observe the sessions conducted with the children. It proved to be a welcome and effective format.

Figure 2
Questionnaire sent to all parents of Pennycoe's Year 4 children
Blackline master in Appendix

THE ARTS AT YEAR 4
Throughout the school, but particularly at Year 4, we are inviting the participation of parents in programs of painting, literature, music, dance and mime. So that parents may be invited to participate in their areas of interest, please complete this form by writing a comment or placing a tick in the appropriate spaces, as indicated.

Painting

	I'm competent & I'd like to help	I've some skills & I'd like to help	I'm interested
Sketching techniques Pastel usage Oils Knowledge of artists Visiting art galleries			

Are there any other areas of painting to which you could contribute?   Yes/No

Comment: _____

Are there any areas in which you would like to learn more?   Yes/No

Comment: _____

Does your child paint/draw at home? _____

What materials does your child use? _____

What does your child draw? _____

Has your child been to an art gallery with you? _____

Would you like information about the Art Gallery? Each month there is information sent to the school. _____

What would you like your child to gain from painting sessions? Tick your preference/s:
1 A liking for painting/sketching
2 Knowledge about artists
3 An appreciation of another's talents and contribution to the wider community
4 Knowledge of how to paint/sketch

Literature

Poetry

	I'm competent & I'd like to help	I've some skills & I'd like to help	I'm interested
Sharing knowledge of poetry Reading poetry to children Writing poetry Typing poems Answering children's queries about poems Knowledge of Australian poets			

Who is your favourite poet? _____

Stories

	I'm competent & I'd like to help	I've some skills & I'd like to help	I'm interested
Writing stories Reading stories to children Discussing stories Illustrating stories Typing stories for children Sharing knowledge of Australian authors Gaining knowledge of Australian story writers/poets Taking children to the library			

Through contact by phone and by letter, parents were informed that their expertise (developed through work, hobbies or interests), their organisational ability and their enthusiasm for learning would be welcomed in students' learning activities planned in the school curriculum.

Parents were surveyed about the contribution they might like to make to the Year 4 children's arts program (see figure 2, The Arts at Year 4). The Pennycoe home-school connection, initiated with the teachers' support, began to be forged with mothers and fathers, dentists, lawyers, artists, poets, journalists, painters, mechanics, shop owners and home builders. Together they provided children with a diverse and enriched curriculum – and also with encouragement, the prized contribution of parents who come as onlookers.

Structure

The Pennycoe Year 4 arts program for the year was organised into a number of topic segments that each lasted four-to-six weeks. The program plan integrated various arts activities within each segment and also across the segments. However, a different set of parents volunteered for each segment, thereby enabling the school to employ each parent in a number of episodes during that segment, yet limiting each parent's contribution to one particular month or so. Being involved in a concentrated way over a limited time suited the parents well.

Within the segment for which they volunteered, parents took part in:
- One school session with the children, each week
- Two home sessions with the children, per segment (held on a Tuesday or a Thursday evening, and voluntarily attended)
- One workshop per segment
- One excursion per segment.

Parents were assured that a teacher would be present to support every session conducted.

THE HOME-SCHOOL CONNECTION

Monitoring the Project

During each session, two school library assistants each formally observed on a proforma (see figure 3, Pupil Behaviour) the behaviour of (any) six children; had the same children complete a response sheet (see figure 4, Child's Response Sheet); and recorded interviews with the same six (see figure 5, The Child Interview) after the session. The responses of the children guided teaching plans for the subsequent sessions. Moreover, an independent person, a teacher from another school, interviewed the parents to find out about their experiences of the project (see figure 6, Parent Response to the Program, Interview Schedule).

Figure 3
Record form used by Pennycoe's library assistants for observing the behaviour of each child participating in a session conducted by parents
Blackline master in Appendix

Figure 4
Sheet completed by each child after taking part in each session conducted by parents
Blackline master in Appendix

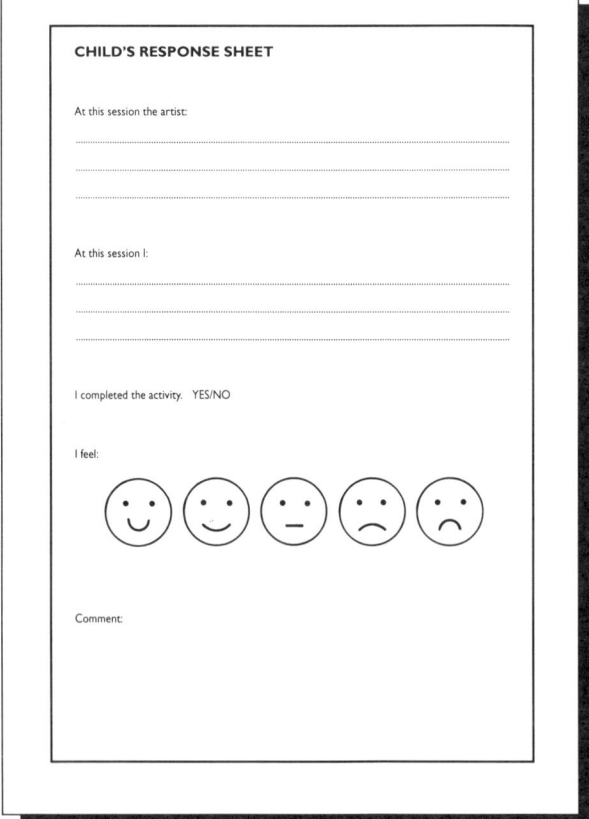

The Outcomes

AFFIRMATION OF LEARNERS AND LEARNING

The school community was proud of its project in using and extending parents' repertoire in helping their children to learn.

A child:

'My Mum taught marbling at another school.'

Parents:

'I'd do it again.'

'The school is to be congratulated on such an initiative.'

'I became confident because I helped the teacher.'

'I think it's great for the parents... there's certainly a lot of talent among the parents.'

'I think if the school has parents with skills that can be converted to the advantage of children, I think the school is wise to involve those parents as much as possible. It is the responsibility of fellow parents to give them the support that any project like this needs in order to

Figure 5
Schedule used by the Pennycoe library assistants to guide and record their interviews with each child to find their response to each session conducted by parents
Blackline master in Appendix

Figure 6
Schedule used by an independent interviewer to guide and record interviews with parents who had participated in the Pennycoe project
Blackline master in Appendix

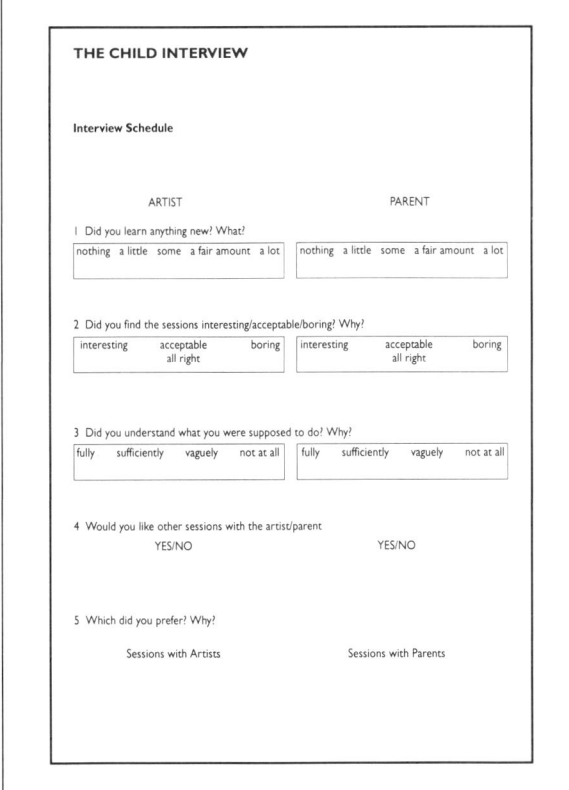

get it going. I use volunteers in my work. We always found that there are some volunteers who are drawers of water and happy to be so to make sure the whole show gets on the road.'

And a teacher's viewpoint:

'Parents can teach what I can't.'

The Pennycoe participants remained alert to the timing, sensitivity and challenge of home-school connecting:

'I think teaching is the province of teachers.'

'The talent has been drawn on... well with teachers you've got your own sort of special strengths and you... teach certain things. There are areas that you neglect. By involving parents you get this source of talent (different knowledge and skill) and that's just great.'

CURRICULUM INNOVATION

Parents introduced new approaches to teaching the curriculum, for example, children were shown how to sketch pictures by using geometric shapes.

INCREASED COMMUNICATION ABOUT CHILDREN'S LEARNING

Parents talked about *what* and *how* children learn, and how parents contribute to children's learning.

INCREASED SOCIAL ACTIVITY

Social events arranged around children's learning drew a strong parent attendance! At the end of the program, of those parents interviewed:

- 68 per cent reported increased communication with the school
- 32 per cent revealed increased confidence in communicating with the school
- 68 per cent revealed an increase in social contact between parents and parents, parents and teachers, and parents and children
- 16 per cent claimed to relate differently with their children as a result of the project
- All parents communicated a changed attitude to the school.

> 'I'm just impressed by the general enthusiasm about it. I get a bit surprised when something like this is offered.'

> 'There has been enjoyment, lots of fun and socialising.'

> 'I think my non-involvement reflects my lack of confidence.'

> 'I think the best thing is the closeness to the children.'

> 'I had time to enjoy the teachers while the children practised with the other parent.'

> 'I ask her (the child) a little more than I used to.'

5
Educational Roles for Parents in Schools

As outlined in chapter 1, parents contribute their competence to the school program in their roles as *spectator, organiser, instructor* and *learner*. This chapter describes the roles more fully and presents examples of the various ways in which parents have adopted these roles in home-school connection programs.

Spectators

In the *spectator* role, parents attend lessons or other sessions conducted in the school, homes or the community in order to observe and encourage children's learning.

Sue Mills, *spectator*
Sue Mills's two children had been at the school for three years. She had always chosen the audience role, happy just to receive information. Because of the enthusiasm of one of her children, she adopted a spectator role in attending both an excursion and a home session. Some months later Sue indicated that she had never really felt part of the school community until her attendance at the excursion and the home session.

Organisers

The *organiser* role is a familiar one for parents in schools – running the tuckshop, changing library books, conducting clothing pools, arranging social events – and one that greatly benefits the school community. Parents working as *organisers* in the home-school *learning* connection, however, directly organise children's *learning*.

In the *organiser* role, parents assist teachers and children but do not teach. They prepare materials, design work sheets and gather other aids in readiness for the lessons whether at school, in the home or in the community. When parents work closely with children in an *organiser* role, they are sensitive to children's needs and encourage children in their efforts.

They also organise the involvement of other parents in similar ventures. Parents as organisers often have little difficulty persuading a friend to join them. Helping out ('I don't want to see you stuck') can change to enthusiastic participation on acquaintance with the experience.

If parents are to work with teachers in classrooms, however, they must accept guidance from the teachers. It must be clear that parents support the teaching plan rather than challenge it. Moreover, organisers are a precious asset only when organisation is needed for learning. Teachers may not appreciate 'organisers' who outstay their function.

Some parent organisers arrange training sessions for other parents. They use the school network effectively – and their own persuasive capacities – to quickly bring together trainers and learners, often even organising the babysitting arrangements!

> **Joy Hass**, *organiser*
> In an initial interview Joy said, ' I wouldn't mind helping – but I couldn't teach the children'. She prepared materials for a school workshop and excursions, and was a most successful encourager of other parents to join the program as *spectators* and *organisers*. Throughout the program Joy maintained the one role of *organiser*. At the end of the program, however, she reported, 'I'd love to paint and, yes, maybe I could teach others craft. I'm good at that.'

Instructors

Researchers find it useful to distinguish between three kinds of parent instructor roles: the *experts* who are usually professionally qualified and practising the knowledge and skills in which they instruct the children –

and who are fluent in its discourse; the *competent* instructors whose competence usually arises from their interests and hobbies – and who often have well developed skills in step-by-step instruction; and the *skilled if trained* instructors who attend training sessions at the school to learn skills which they subsequently teach to the children – and who usually rely on written lesson plans to guide the children's efforts.

Parents as *instructors* extend children's repertoire of knowledge and skills. The *expert* instructors demonstrate to children a relationship between school learning and adult work. The journalist needs to gain facts, plan a report, check the detail and polish his draft before publication; the cook needs knowledge of a recipe, knowledge of how to blend the ingredients and needs time management skills. Children can come to understand success and failure in meeting the demands of a task.

Both *expert* and *competent* instructors usually have a network of colleagues and fellow enthusiasts in the wider community. Access to such networks can give teachers and children information and contact points, including the latest market products of use to schools.

Instructors can also act as mentors, providing the guidance, encouragement and praise with which some students may realise their talents.

The links between school and community, school learning and community work, are made explicit when visiting instructors, whether paid or volunteers – artists, policemen, dancers, journalists, for example – contribute to the school's program. When the instructors are also parents who willingly share time and expertise with students in the school, the linkage of home, school and community is most visible.

Joy Adams, *instructor*

Having attended an information night on the home-school connection program, and read the school information sheet about it, Joy volunteered to teach the children a tarantella, an Italian dance.

At a school session, with the help of the teacher, Joy familiarised the children with the tarantella rhythm. In three subsequent school sessions, she taught them the five basic movements. Joy then ran a training session for interested parents who then reinforced the practice with children at further sessions.

Joy and her trained helpers worked with the children to present a tarantella performance at the school fair. In that task, she worked with other parents who took responsibility for the costuming.

Learners

In the *learner* role, parents acquire skills by attending training sessions arranged through the school. The purpose of such learning can include becoming a *skilled if trained* instructor of children (see above).

Mary McNab, *spectator*, *learner* and *instructor*

Mary attended a home session on poetry as a *spectator*. She took part in a training session on Australian songs, learning two Australian songs, *Carra Barra Wirra Canna* and *Billy of Tea*. She went on to teach these two songs to children at a school session; and then to lead the final segment of a home session where the children sang an Aboriginal lullaby.

More than One Role

It is not uncommon for parents to combine a couple of roles — just as teachers constantly do. In the Pennycoe Project parents were encouraged to extend their role repertoire.

Bob Smith, *instructor* and *organiser*

Bob Smith, an artist and parent of one of the children, agreed to be an instructor in a school session. He was to describe how his painting was influenced by everyday happenings and by his response to his natural surroundings. Bob had prepared a slide presentation showing his view of the misuse of television and of the abuse of natural surroundings.

When explaining to the children how he painted natural scenes, Bob pointed out that it was through keen observation that he interpreted the various hues of colours and the rhythms and patterns in shapes; and combined them to make interesting pictures. Bob showed the children how to mix colours and to paint a Fantasyland using various brush techniques.

As a follow-up to his session as instructor, Bob developed a series of activities for other parents to supervise on an art excursion. He provided considerable detail as he was not able to attend the excursion himself.

THE HOME-SCHOOL CONNECTION

Jim Read, *instructor* and *spectator*

Jim was a journalist who came to the school to show the children how he wrote his sports reports for the local newspaper. At two further sessions in which his wife participated as an organiser, one at home and the other an excursion, Jim took part as a spectator.

On both occasions, the children asked Jim about his work, particularly about the editors, sub-editors and illustrators in whose roles the children had become interested when Jim had described the publication process of the newspaper.

6

Home and Community Settings

The three case stories of this chapter provide some flavour of the experience of home and community sessions undertaken as part of a home-school connection program.

The Hobsons Run an Evening Class

The Hobsons are husband and wife. Jack is a self-taught artist whose hobby is portrait sketching and Mary has a love of Australian poetry which she acquired in her school days. The Hobsons illustrated their interest in the arts in volunteering to take part in the home-school connection project. In their home they taught a group of children confidently and with competence. Their lesson was watched by parents as *spectators*.

In discussion with the teacher, Jack and Mary Hobson prepared the evening session for learning in their home. Jack was to concentrate on sketching and shading techniques. Mary, who had attended school workshop sessions on the works of C J Dennis and on poetry recitation, chose two poems to read to the children: The Sentimental Bloke, by C J Dennis, and The Ballad of the Drover by Banjo Paterson.

The teacher had arranged for the poet, Sally Gramme, who had worked with the children at school, to prepare a tape of some poems that the children had written – as well as of three of her own. The teacher had also prepared printed copies of the children's poems for Mary's use.

The Hobsons had offered to have a group of twelve children to work in their home for the evening. (A similar session was to be held in different homes on other evenings.)

The children were to arrive at 7.00pm. Anne Holt, a parent who had already run a poetry session in her home, was to introduce the session. Mary would then read some poems – after which the children were to illustrate their own poems with the help of Jack. At 8.00pm the evening's learning would conclude with a supper snack – biscuits and cordial for children and coffee for the adults. As a policy, suppers were to be simply prepared and to last no more than a half hour.

Twelve children, four parents as spectators, Anne Holt and the class teacher attended the home session. Anne Holt introduced the session by speaking about the success of a previous session that she had conducted. She then read two poems, based on a schema of C J Dennis, written by some class members.

The Doctor
 I'd like to be a doctor
 and operate on people
at the hospital with the steeple.
I'd look at a few, give them medicine too
And put them in bed
and see they we're fed.
But I wouldn't like to be a doctor
when I have to give people needles
would you?

Swimming Champion
I would like to be a swimmer
And go interstate
I would like to be a winner
and everyone's my mate.
But I wouldn't like to swim
If I couldn't play!
Would you?

Mary then began her poetry segment with the two poems by C J Dennis and Banjo Paterson. Mary gave brief biographic sketches of the two poets to illustrate that poets belong to families and have ordinary lives. Parents and children practised reciting aloud, after Mary, parts of the poems, The Sentimental Bloke and The Ballad of the Drover.

Mary invited the children to listen to the next poems. They were surprised to hear Sally Gramme read *their* poems and some of her own. Both students and parents listened to the poems on the tape and then read them, Mary providing encouragement with:

'That's great!'
'Well done!'
'Try to be a little more confident.'
'Get the swing of the rhythm.'

Next, Mary showed pictures of how the painter, Pro Hart, had illustrated some Australian poems. She distributed copies of the children's own poems and encouraged the children to illustrate their poems. That did not occur! One child wanted to draw the bowl of fruit which was on the table. Other students requested to do likewise. So Jack Hobson adapted his plan to take in their requests.

'Make your orange a bit more of a circle.'
'Keep your pencil at the right angle.'
'Why is it darker underneath?'
'Is your light coming on?'

were some of his comments. He encouraged the children's efforts:

'You've done that correctly.'
'Nice smooth apples over there!'
'That's lovely. Keep going.'

At the conclusion of the session Jack showed the children some of the portraits that he had drawn and told them how he had begun sketching. He used his drawings – and those of the children – to highlight certain art techniques. He emphasised that artists and poets often work together.

The Hobsons' evening session was an enjoyable way of encouraging children in poetry and sketching. The Hobsons said,

'We'll do it again.'

and the children said they'd come again!

Home and Community Settings

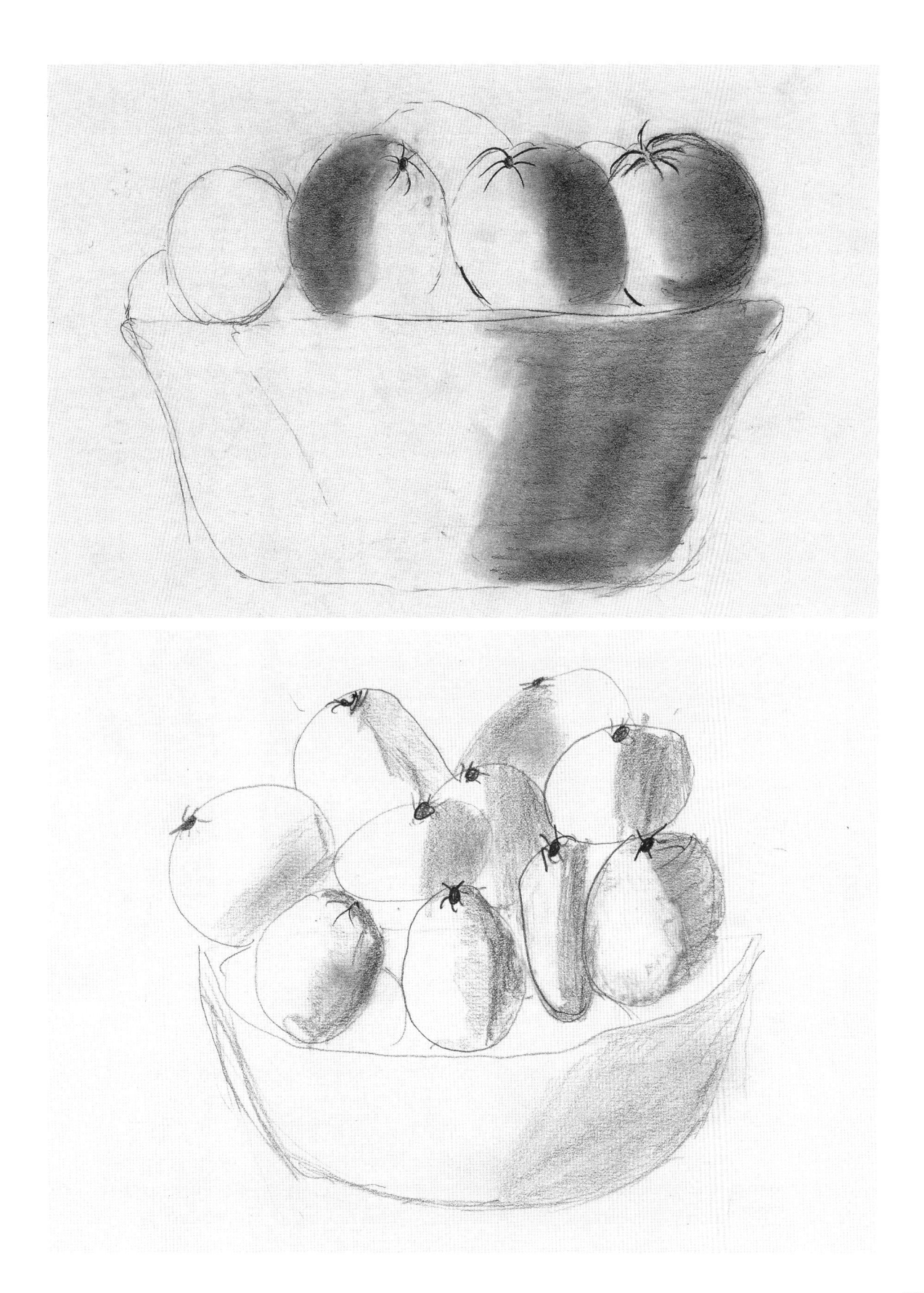

29

THE HOME-SCHOOL CONNECTION

Benita Heddle

Mr Hearne Takes a Year 4 Class
Matthew Hearne is the state manager of a commercial paint firm and works directly on colour making. He met with school staff to discuss his contribution – helping the children to make colour wheels by mixing primary colours. Although the children had not previously made colour wheels, they had practised colour mixing with a parent, an artist, to create imaginary scenes. Matt Hearne would now follow up by showing

the children how colour could be mixed for a different purpose – interior decorating.

Matt conducted a class session, watched by the class teacher and three *spectator* parents. Matt arrived in time to organise the paints and art space; and brought a colour wheel for each of the twenty-five children. He showed the students the colour wheel, described how the colours were made and set the children the task of producing colour wheels similar to the commercial one. Since they could use only primary colours, it was quite a challenging task. Matt suggested that the children commence with filling in the primary colours of the wheel. He then gave clues for making the other colours, for example:

'Blue and yellow make green.'

He also gave instructions:

'Don't use too much water.'

'She doesn't need much red. Red is a strong colour.'

and encouraged the children:

'Yes, that's a lovely one. You have learnt pretty well.'

After the session Matt commented on the children's competencies:

'Some obviously had more skill handling the brush ... others need time with the brushes.'

and also on the nature of the competencies taught in school. He said, in reference to painting within the confined segments of a colour chart:

'Free expression is a lovely thing but sometimes to keep regimented is also a skill to be practised.'

The success of the session was based on Matt's willingness to contribute to students' learning and the students' ready responses to the task.

Matt Hearne considered that he had taught 'a very simple thing' and that the children had learnt it. He commented that while a good teacher is best at holding students' attention, he felt that the children liked someone coming in to teach them something special. He added:

'I have taught them just one thing. Other people have enormous gifts that they can pass on.'

Parents Organise an Art Excursion

Six parents – Sally Green, Anne Brown, Bill Lear, Roger Tait, Sue Reid and Gaye Hass – volunteered to act as either *organisers* or *instructors* for an art excursion for children. Although none of the parents was expert, they had all taken part in training sessions organised by the school and were able to lead the children through a planned set of activities and enjoy a pleasant Saturday afternoon.

On the day, Gaye brought Sue Hamm and another two friends to

THE HOME-SCHOOL CONNECTION

help her. Gaye and Sue had worked together on a previous excursion. The four collected the materials from the school, transported them to the gully and, throughout the afternoon, ensured that the children had the materials they needed.

The other five parents directed the children in four activities using water colours, oils, pastels and writing. The parents used written guidelines (see figure 7, Art Excursion 1, Parent Guide) prepared by a fellow parent, an artist who had previously worked with the same children. However, parents were free to give children whatever guidance they felt was desirable.

The teacher helped with the activities, timed the segments, supervised and enjoyed the afternoon. Sally Green commented:

'What an enjoyable way to learn.'

which seemed to capture the atmosphere of the art session for all parents – even though Roger Tait admitted:

'I really came only to see what would happen.'

Figure 7
Guidelines prepared by a professional artist and parent for use by the parents conducting activities on an art excursion

ART EXCURSION 1
Parent Guide

REALITY/REALISM

ACTIVITY 1
Water Colours
Mr Hatch showed you how to focus on a picture.
Mr Smith and Mr Hearne showed you how to mix colours.
What autumn colours can you see?
Can you see tints?
Be free – big brushes, small brushes.
Use the paint in different ways.
Paint a picture of the gully: the spot you like, for example, the waterfall.

ACTIVITY 2
Oils and Water Colours
Look closely at something – a bush, pl...
Choose the main colour.
Paint the thing of your choice in oil pa...
Choose either a colour you like in you...
painting.

ACTIVITY 3
Writing
How do you feel up here?
Write how you feel.
Tell about the gully.
Describe the gully.

CREATIVITY/IMAGINATION

ACTIVITY 4
Crayons
What shapes can you see?
Cover your page with small shapes like...
**Pause
What is hiding up here?
Outline it in your autumn colours.
**The 'marbling' will occur later.

Figure 8
The list of basic art supplies for an art excursion, suggested by a parent

ART LIST

Item	Sizes	Details
Palette	12" x 1.6"	primed 3/16" masonite
Brushes		
Large	No. 12 or 6cms	e.g., sky, background
Medium	No. 6	e.g., hills, trees, branches
Small	No. 4, 2 & 1	e.g., leaves, flowers, grass
Water Container		
Plastic Bucket	Large household	
Paper		
Size	28 x 38 cms	light or medium cart.
Size	56 x 76 cms	
Colours		primaries
		secondaries
		white
Rags		cleaning up

Home and Community Settings

The gully
I like the gully because of the sound of the water falling down the rocks. The colours around the gully are very beautiful at this time of year. There are lots of leaves on the ground because it's Autumn. The colours are orange and brown and green

The Gully

The gully is a nice, peaceful place with lots of beautiful scenery.
Although you cannot swim in the water, there are lots of different things you can do, for example, you can climb the path to the waterfall.
You can paint a picture of the scenery.
You can find Autumn leaves and you can play amongst the trees.

The Parrot
One day I saw a little parrot sitting in a tree.
He flew away as soon as he saw me.
Then he flew into his nest.
Just to take a little rest.
At that moment he saw a worm,
He grabbed it with his shiny beak.
And watched it squirm.

THE HOME-SCHOOL CONNECTION

> **ART EXCURSION 2**
> Parent Guide
>
> It is necessary to concentrate on the specifics.
> Don't make topic choice too wide or too open.
>
> Special things to look for:
>
> **Reflections**
> • Patterns in the water
> • Colours of the water
> • Light area/shadow area
> • What do you see in the light area, the shadow area?
>
> **Colours and Patterns**
> • Colours in the bark of trees
> • Different greens
> • Patterns/colours between leaves
>
> **Imaginative Response**
> • Imagine you are something you see
> • Paint how you feel
>
> **Poetry**
> Write a poem about the river – trees – noises – feelings
> Example:
> Goldfish
> Oh!
> Wet
> Pet

Figure 9
Guidelines prepared by a professional artist and parent, Bob Smith, and a professional poet, Sally Gramme, for use by the parents conducting activities on an art excursion

Ducks
Oh!
Noisy
Greedy
Pretty Clean
Wet
Ducks

The river
look!
slim;
Quiet peaceful
slow
river

36

PART 2
Making the Connection

7
Creating the Climate

Teachers in schools recognise the need for connecting school learning with home learning and community activities. They are accustomed to discussing children's interests and choosing ideas and activities which motivate them. They spend time informing, showing, advising and asking parents about children's learning needs and progress. The home-school connection is really advanced, however, when home, school and community gain greater understanding of the contributions each makes to children's learning and share this understanding.

A Climate of Confidence
A climate of confidence and trust between home and school is developed if the parties:
1 Affirm each other's contribution (to children's learning)
2 Build a successful repertoire
3 Specify roles and procedures
4 Ensure participation is open to all.

AFFIRM EACH OTHER'S CONTRIBUTION
Teachers affirm the parental contribution to children's school learning when they acknowledge:
- Children are precious family members. Teachers value the care, friendship and respect created in families and continue reinforcing these values.

- Families provide food, shelter, security, comfort, love and challenge for children. A child who is tired and hungry is unable to concentrate on school work.
- Parents spend more time with their children than do teachers. Moreover, parents are constantly reinforcing children's school learning. Parental supervision of homework and music practice, organisation of study times and provision of transport to and from sport, all demonstrate how parents understand the learning process and give liberally of their time and energy to support it.
- Parents guide and encourage their children's achievement.
- Parents provide children with opportunities and experiences on which teachers are able to draw in school learning: for instance, visits to zoos, galleries, museums and historic sites.
- Parents patiently spend many hours clarifying issues with their children. Some children take time to think about things before questions arise for them. Bedtime can be that vital time when an answer becomes the nightcap!

Parents affirm the school's role in their children's learning when:
- They ensure that children get to school on time.
- They provide books, materials, excursion fees, etc., as suggested by the school, in spite of the demands on the family budget.
- They buy toys, books and equipment that support school learning, e.g., the pillar box for posting shapes, story books, encyclopaedias and computers.
- They not only organise study time, a feat in itself in some families, but arrange further learning activities such as sport, dancing and music.
- They (invariably) emphasise to their children the opportunities afforded by education – especially the ones they might have missed.
- They accept guidelines suggested by the school, for instance, on celebration of birthday parties, or hearing a child read. Schools often suggest guidelines in response to parents' requests for guidance.
- They encourage their children to extend their friendship to their school mates and to care for them. The friendship bonds of schools can last a lifetime.

BUILD A SUCCESSFUL REPERTOIRE

The gradual accumulation of a set of successful experiences creates confidence in initiatives of a similar kind. People are attracted to developments that affirm their previous achievements and build on them. By contrast, they are inclined to resist initiatives which they feel might displace them or devalue their previous contribution!

First steps, such as the ones listed below, can be easy ones. The important focus for the home-school connection is children's learning. Even at this early stage, it is helpful to build the repertoire around the parent roles of *spectator*, *organiser*, *instructor* and *learner*. If the early experiences of parental contribution to school learning cover a good range, subsequent initiatives are likely to attract the participation of a wide range of parents.

Even if the school never develops a formal home-school connection program, individual teachers or a small group of teachers can put the following introductory activities to good use.

Introductory Activities
- Invite a few parents (separately) as guest speakers on topics in which they have expertise and which are related to the curriculum plan.
- Invite parents (a few at a time) to observe some lessons in a subject in which they could later help. Give them an observation sheet to complete, so that their observation is directed to issues you wish to emphasise.
- To introduce parents to the four key roles in which they could contribute to the children's learning, invite them to observe sessions in which a particular role is demonstrated.
- Invite parents (in small groups) to a school session to learn a technique which they will use with the children later.
- Invite parents to commence their *organiser* or *instructor* roles by helping a single child, or a small group in the class, with one brief activity.
- Ask a few parents to draw upon their hobbies or interests to teach the children a specialist skill that is related to the children's learning program.
- Plan to include at least some parental contribution in just one lesson per week.

SPECIFY ROLES AND PROCEDURES

Who will do what? Fear, apprehension and threat are often associated with facing any unknown. In the early days of the home-school connection both parents and teachers can experience such feelings. Parents can be worried that if they can't or don't participate, their children will become isolated at school. Teachers can be concerned that parents will be interfering or that competitiveness among parents will be stressful. Fear and apprehension should be acknowledged and discussed if they are to be overcome.

Specifying the context, possible roles and necessary procedures for parental contribution is essential to reducing apprehension, developing confidence in the home-school connection, and appreciating it as attainable and enjoyable. The following issues should be clarified at the outset.

THE HOME-SCHOOL CONNECTION

- The school is responsible for managing the curriculum and ensuring that everyday school activities take their normal course. Parent involvement supports, but does not interrupt, the school program, student learning and the teacher's role and responsibilities.
- The school decides how much and what kind of parental contribution will support children's school learning roles at different times.
- The school commits itself to providing a range of roles for parents and to extending the parents' repertoires of roles so that the children benefit from the many skills possessed by the parent group.
- The home-school connection takes time to establish. The roles given to parents, the tasks set and the teachers' contribution are organised according to:
  - previous experience
  - time for organisation and planning
  - acceptability and enjoyment by those involved.

ENSURE PARTICIPATION IS OPEN TO ALL

Everyone in the school community should be acknowledged as having a part to play in the school's development. With single-class initiatives it is crucial that all the parents are informed of, and welcomed to take part in, the initiative (see figure 10, the Flyer). With a school-wide initiative, all school committees must be given information and, where possible, be represented in prior discussion of and planning for the home-school connection.

WE NEED YOU!

Parents contribute to our school in many ways. You organise social events such as barbecues, dinner dances and coffee parties which raise funds for equipment. You run tuckshop. You attend our many functions arranged for highlighting children's progress: the school concert, parent nights, sport events. In all these activities your efforts are appreciated. Now we need you in some new roles!

- We need Organisers who:
  - Help teachers plan interesting learning activities for children at school, home and at work shops
  - Take materials to excursion sites
  - Assist with distribution of learning materials at school lessons.

- We need instructors who can demonstrate a skill and show the value of acquiring it.

- We need Learners who are willing to attend training sesions in order to master a skill and then teach it to the children.

Be sure to read the newsletter for more information. We invite you to be an organiser, instructor and learner of a skill to help the children.

Direct your enquiries to:
- The Principal
- The Year 4 teachers.

Figure 10
A flyer informs all parents of the class that their help would be appreciated

Management

TIME

In creating a climate for home-school connecting, teachers may need to develop some further capacities for flexibility. Teachers are usually highly skilled in adapting to interruptions, to changes in children's motivational levels, to changes in the timetable caused by sports events, music festivals and local celebrations. Teachers often invite a new baby to be admired in the classroom, at a time that suits Mum. However, home-school connecting can really challenge a teacher's expertise in classroom management.

Definite times have to be appointed and maintained if parents are to work with children. Teachers need time for discussing lesson formats, for setting tasks and for clarifying expected outcomes with parents; for preparing guides and lesson formats for parents to use during lessons. It takes time to explain the unique learning dynamics of each classroom; and to explain the teacher's role in disciplining the students if and when necessary. It takes time, too, to consider these issues.

SPACE

Parents working with children during school time are under teachers' supervision. It is often necessary to negotiate space with other class teachers so that effective supervision can occur.

Figure 11
Times have be to appointed and maintained

Dear Parents

MUSIC PROGRAM
In the music segment of the Year 4 Arts program, we intend that the children should gain an appreciation of history through song, enjoy singing and learning songs and recognise and practise rhythm patterns.

Your participation in the 4-week segment would involve commitment to the following schedule of sessions.

TRAINING
The training session will be held on two occasions. You must attend the training session if you wish to be an organiser or instructor in this segment of the program. Other parent helpers are welcome to attend.

WHERE
School music room.

CHILDREN'S PROGRAM
School session   Thursday 11 October, 11.00am–12.30pm
Home Sessions   Tuesday 16 October, 7.00pm–8.00pm
                              Thursday 18 October, 7.00pm–8.00pm
Excursion   Saturday 20 October, 1.00pm–4.00pm

PARENT HELPERS
Spectators   Welcome to all sessions
Organisers   Must attend the training session
                       Need to give half-an-hour or so before and after the session in which you are organiser
Instructors   At the training session we will decide which segment you will teach.
                       Note all the session dates above.
Learners   You can learn a skill at one of the training sessions!

If you are interested in taking part in the music segment of our home-school connection program, come to the training session. Please return the slip below by Monday 9 September.

Principal

MUSIC PROGRAM
Training Session for Parents
☐ I'll be attending the workshop on Monday 4 October.
☐ I'll be attending the workshop on Thursday 7 October.
☐ Although I will not be attending the training session, I'd like to take part in the October Music Program as a Spectator.

Name _____ Telephone _____

8
Training Sessions

It is commonplace in schools that a minority of 'enthusiastic' parents are the regular participants in school activities, are known and regarded favourably by the teachers, and are skilled and assured in their dealing with the school (Toomey, 1980). The other parents, often perceived wrongly as apathetic towards their children's schooling, usually lack confidence in their dealings with the schools.

If the home-school connection is to extend to the second, larger, group of parents, schools need to extend the educational enterprise to include parents as learners. Even parents who are confident in their relationship with the school may benefit from training sessions that equip them for unfamiliar roles.

As a result of short training sessions, parents can:
- Give and gain insights into the school curriculum, e.g., parents demonstrate a painting technique; parents are shown by the teacher how the children are taught to spell.
- Master specific knowledge and skills, e.g., the importance of rhythm in song; brush techniques in painting.
- Learn new teaching strategies and techniques, e.g., how to assist children with their reading; how to help them learn tables through song.
- See how other parents contribute to the school learning of children, e.g., through observing how other parents prepare teaching

materials, work as a team, and provide encouragement to children.
- Develop confidence and experience in connecting with the school through adopting various *spectator*, *organiser*, *instructor* and *learner* roles.
- Extend children's 'school' learning outside the classroom through, e.g., observation of colour in a natural setting, noting of changes in prices in the supermarket, and reflecting on the day's achievements.

Who's Responsible for Training?

It is the school, after consultation with parents, that is responsible for deciding what training it can offer parents, along with when and how the training will be provided. The school possesses the teaching expertise for organising how best to teach parents the knowledge and skills they are interested in acquiring. Parents decide whether or not to accept each opportunity.

Some parents will require little or no training for the tasks they undertake. Some are already competent and skilled in the area in which they will teach. However, the teachers, who are responsible for the organisation of students' school learning, need to know exactly what content and processes are planned by the parent. Discussion of the parent's plans, well in advance, is an absolutely necessary procedure. During such discussion, teachers might suggest modifications to the plan in the interests of improved learning for the children.

If a school decides to run a training session or program for parents, a teacher needs to be in attendance to see what the parents learn and to gauge their reactions; and to assess how well the sessions are working.

Figure 12
The school decides what training it can offer to parents

Dear Parents

DRAMA PROGRAM
As outlined in previous letters, the Year 4 Arts program during July and August will emphasise drama based on everyday happenings.

You are invited to take part in a workshop session for parents. The workshop session will run twice.

When?
Monday 16 June and Thursday 19 June
7.00pm to 8.30pm

Where?
The school's multi-purpose building.

At these sessions we will discuss the goals of the drama program, the specific learning experiences planned for the children and how parents can help with activities to build the children's self-esteem.

The session will be conducted by Mrs Brand, a parent and drama teacher, and me, the Principal.

The program will be interesting as we will use games such as *Give and Take* to teach you techniques for encouraging the children.

Please return the slip below by Friday 13 June.

Thanks for your contribution to the home-school connection program.

Principal

DRAMA WORKSHOP FOR PARENTS

☐ I'll be attending the workshop on Monday 16 June
☐ I'll be attending the workshop on Thursday 19 June.

Name _____ Telephone _____

Who Does the Training?

Training programs for parents require commitment by teachers. However, while teachers may well take sessions concerned with teaching and learning strategies and techniques, they don't have to *conduct* all the training.

Teachers can organise community members and parents with expertise and skills to conduct sessions. In training sessions these people demonstrate not only their own expertise but also (if need be, with the help of a teacher) how their expert territory might best be approached by novices.

When training sessions are taken by parents, teachers and other parents are both learners. This factor can itself reduce barriers and apprehension experienced by some parents, give teachers the enjoyment of a class learner role, and generate fun and relaxation. Teachers don't have a monopoly on expertise!

Training can be jointly done by parent and teacher. Bob Smith, a parent who was an artist by occupation, prepared guidelines for children's art sessions on how to achieve reflections and other light effects when painting water, and how to gain an appearance of texture in the painting of trees. The teacher met with Bob, and subsequently led parents and another teacher through a training session on these techniques, in preparation for an excursion to the river.

Training Modes

LECTURE

Information is given to parents who have the opportunity to ask questions thus gaining clarification of issues.

> A lecture on observation technique emphasised how parents can help their children become observant through taking time to interact with the children in their observations of such everyday experiences as colour, texture, feelings, reactions, and preferences. Parents were encouraged to restate four questions with their children:
> - What do I see?
> - What does it mean to me?
> - Does this remind me of another experience or image?
> - How do I appreciate this?

WORKSHOP

Participants practise skills under guidance and in cooperation with others. Many workshops are group learning sessions.

> Poet, Sally Gramme, was experienced in writing children's poetry and in poetry recitation. She explained different schema in poetry, and illustrated these in the work of Australian poets. The parents practised poetry recitation under Sally Gramme's guidance, in preparation for home sessions when parents would guide children's poetry recitation.

OBSERVATION

Participants observe behaviour, focusing on chosen elements.

Under the guidance of teachers, parents and children work together to solve a problem such as mapping the route for an excursion. Parents are to observe the child's perspective and to bring these observations to a discussion that immediately follows the observation session.

> Gaye Hass and Sue Hamm, parents of Year 4 children, attended a school art workshop. They observed how the teacher organised the children to use paper shapes to make a collage background for an animal picture. Gaye and Sue attended the workshop as observers so that they could act as competent organisers for an art excursion the following Saturday.

DEMONSTRATION

One person (or several) shows others how to do something.

Teachers are skilled in strategies and techniques for helping children to learn, e.g., motivating, demonstrating, questioning, practice and consolidation. A teacher can show parents how to use one or several techniques that will enhance parents' teaching skills.

> Valda White, parent of a Year 4 child, attended a school session to learn the technique of marbling. One of the school's teachers was the instructor. In three art sessions that followed, she taught the children how to marble in different ways.

Timing of Sessions

Training sessions need not be lengthy. An hour-long session can fulfil a parent's need. It is important, though, to schedule sessions at times that are convenient to parents. In the Pennycoe Project the most popular times for training sessions were the hour before children's dismissal from school, and at 5pm.

In the Pennycoe experience, some training sessions were held too close to the time when parents were to use the skills they had learnt. It is important to allow sufficient time between training and 'performance' for parents to consolidate skills through practice and questioning.

9
Discussion Program for the School Community

All previous chapters of this book show how to extend the usual scope of parental contribution to children's learning into richer school learning experiences. Individual teachers, groups of teachers or a whole school can use the ideas and activities discussed in this book as single events, a series of events, termly activities, etc., without using a discussion program.

A discussion program has advantages, however. The principles and practice underpinning the home-school connection can be publicised and shared with all who attend the meeting. Roles and procedures are discussed, clarified and make explicit in an atmosphere that is open and non-threatening. Experiences can be shared, worries aired and understandings reached together.

Through a format of presentation, group discussion and reporting in a single session or over a series of sessions, the parents and teachers of a class or school come to better appreciate:
- How children learn
- How the home-school connection strengthens and enriches children's learning
- How parental expertise can contribute to the school program

- The *educational* roles for parents in schools
- Community responsibility for children's learning
- Parents' attitudes to involvement in the school program
- Parents' desired level of involvement in the school program
- The nature of parents' interests and talents
- How the parent contribution to children's learning can be promoted
- Ways of forming closer liaison between home and school.

Other outcomes of the Discussion Program can include:
- New approaches to the home-school connection
- More parents volunteering their services
- A curriculum being injected with new activities
- Stronger partnerships between the home and the school
- Participative decision making for the home-school connection.

The Program

The Discussion Program should commence with an introductory session which welcomes parents and provides them with information about the Program's goals, content, sequence, format, style, and procedures. The introductory session should clarify guidelines for group participation; and settle on times and places for each session. A suggested format for this introductory session is provided later in this chapter.

Such information not only gives parents a helpful overview at this stage, but also allows them to choose which sessions to attend. Although the Discussion Program has a sequence, parents should be able to attend one, a few or all sessions.

The topics for subsequent sessions can be based on the previous chapters of this book. The content of each chapter provides briefing on the topic for the presenter. Discussion Starters, (figures 17-24) are also based on each chapter. In the Appendix the Discussion Starters are presented as blackline masters for making either overhead transparencies for the presentation or handouts for distribution to the groups.

The Discussion Program might comprise hour-long sessions with one (chapter) topic per session – a pattern that has been used successfully in a number of cases. Alternatively, the discussions could be held over fewer – but longer – sessions.

PROGRAM ORGANISATION

Decide the structure and timing of the program. Generate some curiosity and anticipation in the school community.

Publicise the program, including venue and starting time, to parents through:

- Announcements at a school function
- The school newsletter or a special flyer
- Various school and parent group meetings
- The 'grapevine'.

Prepare the space. A successful discussion program depends on intelligent organisation of the space. Participants will feel welcome if organisers:
- Ensure that the space created is comfortable and interesting
- Plan to accommodate a few unexpected participants
- See that each group has sufficient space so that the dynamics of its discussion are not interrupted by those of other groups. But enthusiastic outbursts are welcomed!
- Have an overhead projector for group use
- Prepare for a tea or coffee break.

Figure 13
A sheet for monitoring parents' response to the Discussion Program
Blackline master in Appendix

Monitor the program. To obtain feedback, essential for future planning:
- During and after each session allow participants to comment on the program.
- Ask participants to complete a Comment Sheet (see figure 13) for each session of the discussion program.
- Keep the format of the Comment Sheet simple.

PROGRAM PRESENTATION

The presenter(s) of the Discussion Program will:
- Have a clear knowledge of the program goals (see figure 14).
- Plan the content and format of each session
- Plan for the number of groups (no more than eight people in each)
- Prepare a handout sheet describing the responsibilities for the roles

of group leader, timekeeper, scribe and spokesperson; and providing guidelines for group discussion. See figure 16, Guidelines for Group Participation.
- Prepare the overhead transparencies
- Decide the time limit for each segment of each session
- Practise the presentation
- Allow sufficient time for feedback
- Aim to be flexible and sensitive to the need for change in arrangements if necessary.

After each session they will:
- Collate and analyse responses from the Comment Sheets
- Keep responses in mind when planning future sessions.

At the end of the Discussion Program they will:
- Recommend action
- Publicise the action.

Introductory Session

Conducting an introductory session allows participants to become familiar with the content and format of the program. An introductory session can be held in the form of an information night and/or afternoon. Here is a suggested format for presenting the introductory session.

PRESENTATION

1 Welcome

2 Background to the Program

   Parents and school staff are recognised as educators of children. So are members of the community. Policemen, artists, poets and dramatists formally visit our school to assist in the school program. We also arrange school excursions in order to expand school learning experiences.

   Parents work within the community and provide services to the community, which also can be beneficial to schools. If the school knows what parent expertise, interest, and willingness is available, it can invite parents to contribute to school learning activities.

   The school can provide training programs for parents to master certain skills so that they can competently and confidently contribute to expanding children's learning experiences. Successful training sessions have been held during school time (the final hour before dismissal proved particularly popular), and in the evening.

   Interesting findings from other schools' experience of this kind of home-school connection are:
   - Children learnt skills which the school staff would not have taught.
   - Parents influenced the curriculum.
   - Communication and social contact between parents, teachers and students increased.

3 Program Goals

   Use an overhead transparency. See figure 14, Program Goals, for a model.

4 Program Content and Sequence

   Use an overhead transparency. See figure 15, Program Content and Sequence, for a model.

5 Program Format, Style and Procedures

   Although the Discussion Program is designed as a sequence, each session is complete in itself. Parents can attend one, a few or all sessions planned by the school.

   The sequence for each discussion session is:
   - Presentation of information on the topic
   - Group discussion of particular aspects of the topic
   - Feedback from groups.

THE HOME-SCHOOL CONNECTION

PROGRAM GOALS

1 Use parental expertise in the school program.

2 Extend the roles which parents undertake in helping their children learn.

3 Extend children's learning beyond

4 Enhance community acceptance

PROGRAM CONTENT AND SEQUENCE

Introductory Information Session

Parents and Schools

All Parents and Teachers

Education for Living

The Pennycoe Project

Roles for Parents in Schools

Home and Community Settings

Creating the Climate

Training Sessions

Figure 14
Program goals are presented on an overhead transparency.
Blackline master in Appendix

Figure 15
An overhead transparency displays the content and sequence of the Discussion Program.
Blackline master in Appendix

Each session of the Discussion Program is planned to meet the needs of the teachers and parents. The presenter suggests the issues for discussion but the group can replace the suggested issues with ones it regards as more relevant.

6 Guidelines for Group Participation

Speak to the Guidelines. See figure 16, Guidelines for Group Participation, for a model handout. Figure 16 could also be prepared as two OHTs.

7 Size and Composition of Groups

Discussion groups should comprise no more than eight participants. One teacher working with six or seven parents works well. (If a class teacher is working alone with parents, it is essential that the solo teacher spend time with each group.)

8 Duration of Sessions

An hour or so is suggested.

7 Venues for Sessions

Sessions will be held in the school. However, follow-up sessions can be planned in other venues, for example, in homes or as suggested by the participants.

2 DISCUSSION

The presenter assures those at the introductory session that the Discussion Program is a time of learning together; and then invites the participants to form groups of no more than eight members, in specified locations.

The presenter, on this first occasion, will have prepared a sufficient number of people to take on the role of group leader – preparation which could be maintained or discarded in further sessions, depending on the confidence, competence and desires of participants to elect, and perform as, group leaders.

The group leaders will ensure that the other three group positions are taken up, distribute Guidelines for Group Participation, and lead the group in discussion (see figure 16).

At a specified time, the groups will come together again to hear each group's spokesperson present the group's suggestions and responses.

The presenter concludes the session with a summary and notice of further sessions.

Subsequent Sessions

The subsequent sessions can be based on the chapters of this book. Presenters can brief themselves by reading the appropriate chapter. Each of the Discussion Starters (figures 17 to 24) is also based on one chapter of this book. In the Appendix, the eight Discussion Starters are presented as blackline masters for making either overhead transparencies for presentation or handouts for distribution to the groups.

The sessions can be held over eight, hour-long, sessions or over fewer but longer sessions.

As parents should be able to attend one, a few or all sessions, the sessions need to be organised to meet that diversity of experience. Presenters and group leaders need to keep in mind that the experience of the Discussion Program will vary among participants.

Discussion Program for Teachers

With some adapting of the content of the *Discussion Starters*, the content of this chapter has been successfully used with groups of teachers, principals and educational consultants, as a professional development program on the Home-School Connection.

GUIDELINES FOR GROUP PARTICIPATION

All Participants
☆ Express their own expectations and hopes for the home-school connection
☆ Acknowledge appreciation of other people's ideas
☆ Focus on the set task
☆ Listen to what others see is the task
☆ Encourage others to present their ideas
☆ Appreciate 'thinking time'
☆ Try to summarise the responses of other group members
☆ Try to summarise the overall group response.

The Group Leader
maintains a focus on the task, encouraging the active participation of each member.

The Group Timekeeper
ensures that the group works within the established time frame.

The Group Scribe
records the ideas expressed by participants.

The Group Spokesperson
presents the group's suggestions and responses to the meeting.

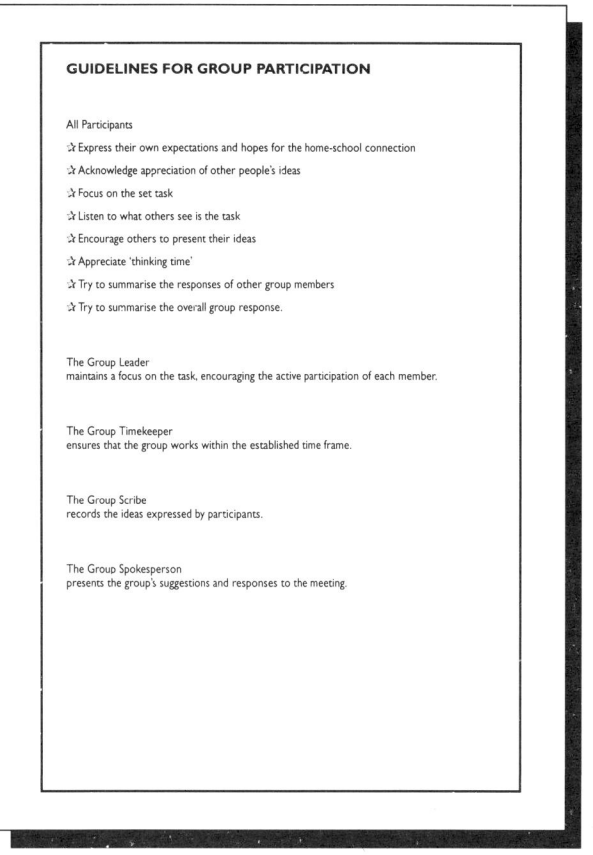

Figure 16
Each participant receives a copy of the guidelines for group participation.
Blackline master in Appendix

Figure 17 Discussion Starter 1 *Blackline master in Appendix*

PARENTS AND SCHOOLS

☆ Parents and teachers share responsibility for children's learning.

☆ The school encourages parents to taken an active interest in their children's progress.

☆ Parents adopt many roles in schools.

☆ What is the school policy on parent participation?

☆ What supportive roles do parents exercise?
  • tuckshop
  • school board

☆ What educational roles do parents have?
  • correctors of writing
  • helpers with reading

☆ What proportion of the parents in our school would act as spectators, instructors or learners in our school?

☆ Which role appeals to you? Why?

Figure 18 Discussion Starter 2 *Blackline master in Appendix*

ALL PARENTS ARE TEACHERS

☆ Parents teach their children:
  • First words
  • Personal hygiene
  • Safety rules
  • Values
  • Social skills

☆ Parents teach by encouragement, demonstration, modelling, revising and monitoring children's efforts.

☆ What can you tell the school about the way your child learns?

☆ What proud memories do you have of teaching your child?

☆ What do schools expect parents to teach school-age children?

☆ In what do you find the school's expectations challenging and/or burdensome?

☆ Parents and teachers perform complementary roles in educating school-age children.

Figure 19 Discussion Starter 3 *Blackline master in Appendix*

EDUCATION FOR LIVING

☆ Learning takes places everywhere that a child is.

☆ Education for Living involves the home, school and community.

☆ Parents and teachers reinforce the importance of gaining knowledge and skills for living.

☆ In what ways are you as parents presently educating your children for living?

☆ When are you initiators, facilitators, instructors or encouragers of learning for living? Give specific examples.

☆ What living skills would you like the school to develop now?

☆ Through what community experiences and excursions could the school extend children's learning?

☆ Make suggestions for an excursion in which children can practise a skill and learn a skill.

Figure 20 Discussion Starter 4 *Blackline master in Appendix*

THE PENNYCOE PROJECT

☆ Parents can help provide a diverse and enriched curriculum for students.

☆ Personal contact influences parent participation.

☆ Parents are willing to be involved in schools in a concentrated way over a limited time.

☆ What kinds of occupational expertise could parents contribute to school learning programs?

☆ What hobbies, interests and ideas can you share with students?

☆ What value do you see in Pennycoe school initiatives?

☆ How does parental involvement at Pennycoe compare with parental activity at our school?

☆ What program can you initiate to involve parents?

Figure 21 Discussion Starter 5 *Blackline master in Appendix*

EDUCATIONAL ROLES FOR PARENTS IN SCHOOLS

☆ Different roles have distinct characteristics.

☆ The roles of *spectator, learner* and *instructor* focus on children's learning.

☆ Parents and teachers combine roles when assisting students.

☆ What aspects of the case studies are familiar to our school?

☆ What school activities involve you as *learners, instructors* and *organisers*?

☆ What role would you like to develop? Why?

☆ Tell how you could adopt two of these three roles: *spectator, learner, instructor*.

Figure 22 Discussion Starter 6 *Blackline master in Appendix*

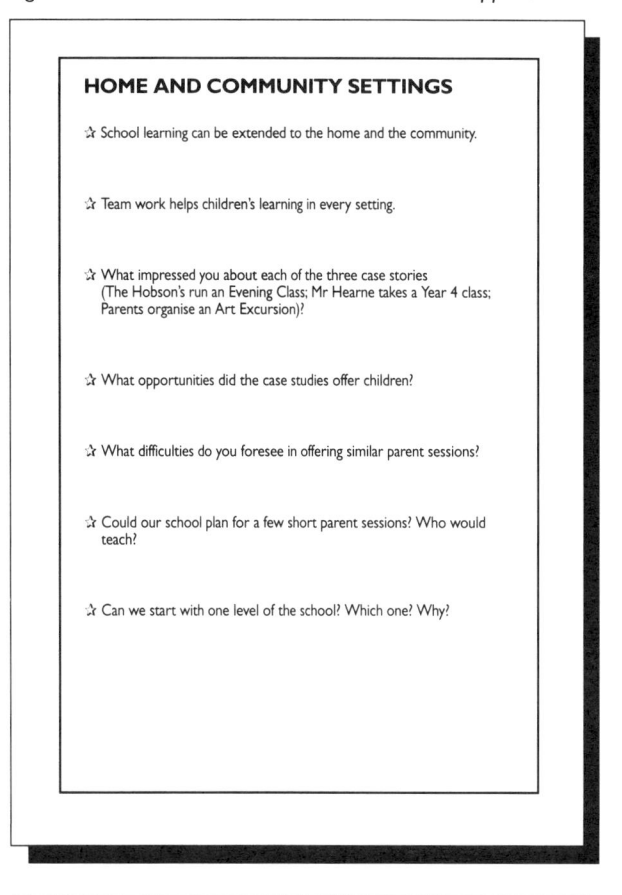

HOME AND COMMUNITY SETTINGS

☆ School learning can be extended to the home and the community.

☆ Team work helps children's learning in every setting.

☆ What impressed you about each of the three case stories (The Hobson's run an Evening Class; Mr Hearne takes a Year 4 class; Parents organise an Art Excursion)?

☆ What opportunities did the case studies offer children?

☆ What difficulties do you foresee in offering similar parent sessions?

☆ Could our school plan for a few short parent sessions? Who would teach?

☆ Can we start with one level of the school? Which one? Why?

Figure 23 Discussion Starter 7 *Blackline master in Appendix*

CREATING THE CLIMATE

☆ Parents and teachers affirm the contributions of each other to children's learning.

☆ In our school, when do parents tell the teachers about their children's progress and interests at home?

☆ In our school, when do teachers tell the parents about children's progress and interests at school?

☆ What encourages you to feel confident to share information about your child with the teachers? What encourages you to entrust that information to the teacher?

☆ The school is responsible for children's learning within the school program. Parental contribution to the school program is always at the school's invitation?

☆ How could you extend other parents' repertoires of roles so that the children benefit?

☆ Make suggestions of the contributions that you (or a small group of parents) could make to a specific class. Suggest the time and space needed.

Figure 24 Discussion Starter 8 *Blackline master in Appendix*

TRAINING SESSIONS

☆ Training programs can equip parents for unfamiliar roles.

☆ Only a small number of parents presently contributes to learning activities at our school.

☆ Training sessions increase parent involvement.

☆ Parents and teachers are learners.

☆ What training is provided by the school for you?

☆ In what areas have you recently asked for help? Do other parents want this too?

☆ Which training formats appeal to you: lecture, workshop, observation, demonstration?

☆ Suggest some specific training sessions for a group of parents to enable them to help their children's learning.

☆ Work out a simple time frame for such training and practice over a one-month period.

10

Curriculum Plan

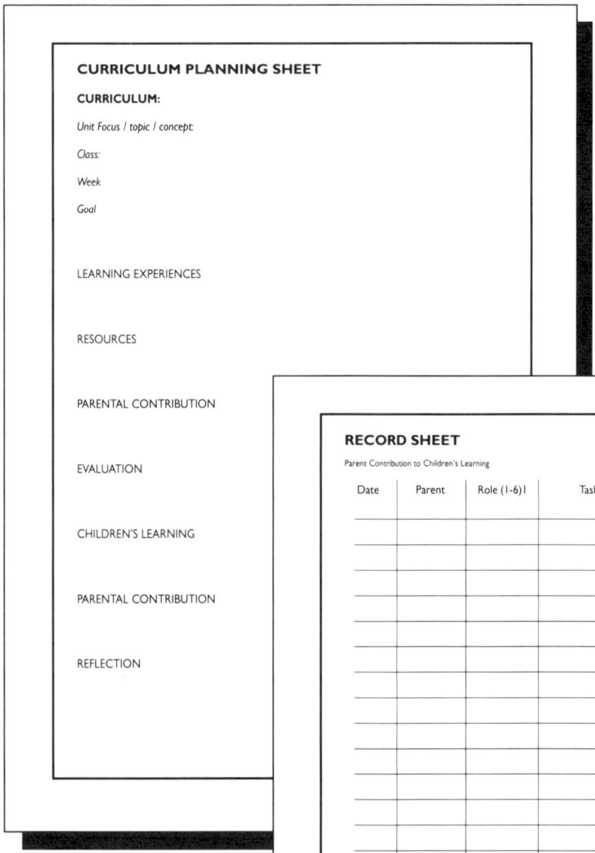

CURRICULUM PLANNING SHEET

CURRICULUM:

Unit Focus / topic / concept:

Class:

Week

Goal

LEARNING EXPERIENCES

RESOURCES

PARENTAL CONTRIBUTION

EVALUATION

CHILDREN'S LEARNING

PARENTAL CONTRIBUTION

REFLECTION

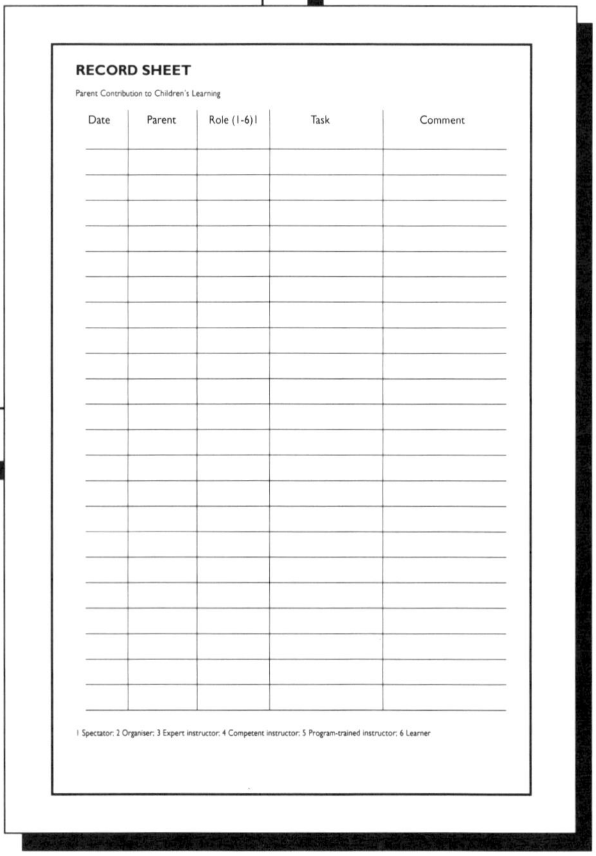

RECORD SHEET

Parent Contribution to Children's Learning

Date	Parent	Role (1-6)1	Task	Comment

1 Spectator; 2 Organiser; 3 Expert instructor; 4 Competent instructor; 5 Program-trained instructor; 6 Learner

Figure 25
A proforma for planning each curriculum segment
Blackline master in Appendix

Figure 26
A proforma for monitoring parent participation
Blackline master in Appendix

Use of planning and recording sheets, such as those provided as figures 25 and 26 in this chapter, enable teachers to systematically – but quickly – observe, monitor and reflect upon the nature and extent of the parental contribution to class learning; and to decide on the directions in which they wish to shape and extend the parents' contributions to learning.

Teachers can use the Curriculum Planning Sheet (figure 25) to ensure that the parental contribution to children's learning becomes an integral part of their usual planning procedures.

On the Record Sheet (figure 26) teachers or parent organisers can record the type of contribution make by individual parents so that the repertoire of individual parents may be varied and extended if they so wish. Every parent can claim success in some facet of teaching, whether it be modelling, telling, explaining, correcting, extending, or encouraging questions; and every parent is an experienced organiser of a child's activities.

PARENT ROLES IN SCHOOLS

Audience

Spectators

Fund raisers

Aides

Organisers

Instructors

Learners

Policy makers

Decision makers

Advocates

Figure 1, page 2, Parent roles in schools
From *The Home-School Connection* by Jacqueline McGilp and Maureen Michael, Eleanor Curtain Publishing, 1994. This page may be reproduced for use in a school discussion program.

THE ARTS AT YEAR 4

Throughout the school, but particularly at Year 4, we are inviting the participation of parents in programs of painting, literature, music, dance and mime. So that parents may be invited to participate in their areas of interest, please complete this form by writing a comment or placing a tick in the appropriate spaces, as indicated.

Painting

	I'm competent & I'd like to help	I've some skills & I'd like to help	I'm interested
Sketching techniques Pastel usage Oils Knowledge of artists Visiting art galleries			

Are there any other areas of painting to which you could contribute?   Yes/No

Comment: _____

_____

Are there any areas in which you would like to learn more?   Yes/No

Comment: _____

_____

Does your child paint/draw at home? _____

What materials does your child use? _____

What does your child draw? _____

Has your child been to an art gallery with you? _____

Would you like information about the Art Gallery? Each month there is information sent to the school. _____

What would you like your child to gain from painting sessions? Tick your preference/s:
1 A liking for painting/sketching
2 Knowledge about artists
3 An appreciation of another's talents and contribution to the wider community
4 Knowledge of how to paint/sketch

Figure 2, page 14, Questionnaire sent to all parents of Pennycoe's Year 4 children
From *The Home-School Connection* by Jacqueline McGilp and Maureen Michael, Eleanor Curtain Publishing, 1994. This page may be reproduced for use in a school discussion program.

Dance

	I'm competent & I'd like to help	I've some skills & I'd like to help	I'm interested
Dancing alone Dancing in a group			

Which is your favourite dance group? _____

Would you like your child to learn dance?   Yes/No

Would be willing to be involved in a dance session?   Yes/No

Music

	I'm competent & I'd like to help	I've some skills & I'd like to help	I'm interested
Playing an instrument Enjoying listening to music Enjoying singing Composing music Attending music concerts Knowing Australian songs			

My favourite music is: _____

Would be willing to be involved in a music segment?   Yes/No

Mime

	I'm competent & I'd like to help	I've some skills & I'd like to help	I'm interested
Knowledge of mime Participation in mime Appreciation of the art of mime			

Would be willing to be involved in a mime segment?   Yes/No

NAME: _____   TELEPHONE NUMBER: _____

Figure 2 cont., page 15, Questionnaire sent to all parents of Pennycoe's Year 4 children
From *The Home-School Connection* by Jacqueline McGilp and Maureen Michael, Eleanor Curtain Publishing, 1994. This page may be reproduced for use in a school discussion program.

Literature

Poetry

	I'm competent & I'd like to help	I've some skills & I'd like to help	I'm interested
Sharing knowledge of poetry Reading poetry to children Writing poetry Typing poems Answering children's queries about poems Knowledge of Australian poets			

Who is your favourite poet? _____

Stories

	I'm competent & I'd like to help	I've some skills & I'd like to help	I'm interested
Writing stories Reading stories to children Discussing stories Illustrating stories Typing stories for children Sharing knowledge of Australian authors Gaining knowledge of Australian story writers/poets Taking children to the library			

Figure 2 cont., page 14, Questionnaire sent to all parents of Pennycoe's Year 4 children
From *The Home-School Connection* by Jacqueline McGilp and Maureen Michael, Eleanor Curtain Publishing, 1994. This page may be reproduced for use in a school discussion program.

PUPIL BEHAVIOUR
Record of observation of six selected children

Session:

Behaviour	Pupil 1	2	3	4	5	6
Raises new issue or topic						
Agrees with speaker						
Gives opinion/expresses feeling						
Asks for opinion or suggestion						
Disagrees						
Shows tension/criticises						
Other						

Figure 3, page 16, Record form used by Pennycoe's library assistants for observing the behaviour of each child participating in a session conducted by parents From *The Home-School Connection* by Jacqueline McGilp and Maureen Michael, Eleanor Curtain Publishing, 1994. This page may be reproduced for use in a school discussion program.

CHILD'S RESPONSE SHEET

At this session the artist:

....

....

....

At this session I:

....

....

....

I completed the activity.   YES/NO

I feel:

☺ ☺ 😐 ☹ ☹

Comment:

Figure 4, page 16, Sheet completed by each child after taking part in each session conducted by parents
From *The Home-School Connection* by Jacqueline McGilp and Maureen Michael, Eleanor Curtain Publishing, 1994. This page may be reproduced for use in a school discussion program.

THE CHILD INTERVIEW

Interview Schedule

ARTIST	PARENT

1 Did you learn anything new? What?

nothing a little some a fair amount a lot	nothing a little some a fair amount a lot

2 Did you find the sessions interesting/acceptable/boring? Why?

interesting acceptable boring all right	interesting acceptable boring all right

3 Did you understand what you were supposed to do? Why?

fully sufficiently vaguely not at all	fully sufficiently vaguely not at all

4 Would you like other sessions with the artist/parent

    YES/NO   YES/NO

5 Which did you prefer? Why?

    Sessions with Artists   Sessions with Parents

Figure 5, page 17, Schedule used by the Pennycoe library assistants to guide and record their interviews with each child to find their response to each session conducted by parents
From *The Home-School Connection* by Jacqueline McGilp and Maureen Michael, Eleanor Curtain Publishing, 1994. This page may be reproduced for use in a school discussion program.

PARENT RESPONSE TO THE PROGRAM
Interview Schedule

1. What involvement have you had in the arts program?
   Probes:
   - Organisation
   - Training
   - Support
   - Presence

2. Would you be willing to continue helping in a project of this kind next year? In what capacity?

3. What would you like to see or not like to see in the future development of this program?

4. Do you think that you have gained or not gained in:
   - Knowledge
   - Skills
   - Attitude

   Do you think that the children have gained or not gained in:
   - Knowledge
   - Skills
   - Attitude

   Comment on what you have heard from your child, or seen.

5. Has this program affected your confidence?
   - As a teacher
   - Using special skills
   - Demonstrating new skills
   - Doing something for the first time
   - Being present at this type of session for the first time

6. Has this program affected the way you relate to your child? Comment.

7. What is your attitude towards the school and teachers because of this program?

8. What is your attitude towards the value of the arts in your child's education?
   - Painting
   - Dance
   - Music
   - Mime

9. Do you feel you were given enough guidance as to how to keep the children learning?

10. What would be your attitude towards expert parents training non-expert parents to conduct sessions?

Figure 6, page 17, Schedule used by an independent interviewer to guide and record interviews with parents who had participated in the Pennycoe project
From *The Home-School Connection* by Jacqueline McGilp and Maureen Michael, Eleanor Curtain Publishing, 1994. This page may be reproduced for use in a school discussion program.

COMMENT SHEET

Session:
Date:

Please give us your comments on these three aspects of the session.

1 The presentation

_____

_____

_____

_____

2 The usefulness of the handout, Discussion Starters

_____

_____

_____

_____

3 The group discussion

_____

_____

_____

_____

Name (optional): _____

Figure 13, page 51, A sheet for monitoring parents' response to the Discussion Program
From *The Home-School Connection* by Jacqueline McGilp and Maureen Michael, Eleanor Curtain Publishing, 1994. This page may be reproduced for use in a school discussion program.

PROGRAM GOALS

1 Use parental expertise in the school program.

2 Extend the roles which parents undertake in helping their children learn.

3 Extend children's learning beyond the school.

4 Enhance community acceptance of responsibility for children's learning.

Figure 14, page 54, Program goals are presented on an overhead transparency.
From *The Home-School Connection* by Jacqueline McGilp and Maureen Michael, Eleanor Curtain Publishing, 1994. This page may be reproduced for use in a school discussion program.

PROGRAM CONTENT AND SEQUENCE

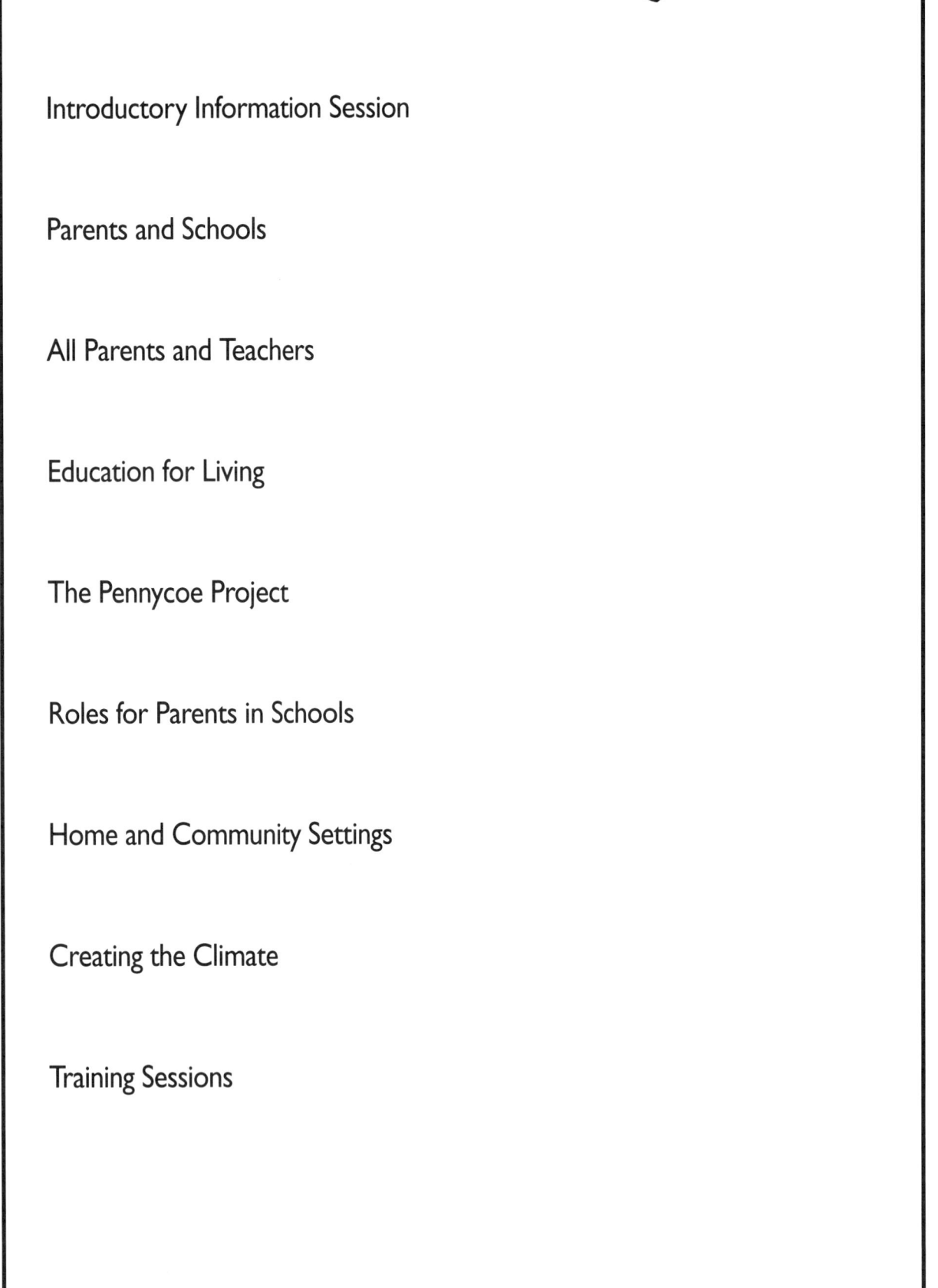

Introductory Information Session

Parents and Schools

All Parents and Teachers

Education for Living

The Pennycoe Project

Roles for Parents in Schools

Home and Community Settings

Creating the Climate

Training Sessions

Figure 15, page 54, An overhead transparency displays the content and sequence of the Discussion Program.
From *The Home-School Connection* by Jacqueline McGilp and Maureen Michael, Eleanor Curtain Publishing, 1994. This page may be reproduced for use in a school discussion program.

GUIDELINES FOR GROUP PARTICIPATION

All Participants

☆ Express their own expectations and hopes for the home-school connection

☆ Acknowledge appreciation of other people's ideas

☆ Focus on the set task

☆ Listen to what others see is the task

☆ Encourage others to present their ideas

☆ Appreciate 'thinking time'

☆ Try to summarise the responses of other group members

☆ Try to summarise the overall group response.

The Group Leader
maintains a focus on the task, encouraging the active participation of each member.

The Group Timekeeper
ensures that the group works within the established time frame.

The Group Scribe
records the ideas expressed by participants.

The Group Spokesperson
presents the group's suggestions and responses to the meeting.

Figure 16, page 55, Each participant receives a copy of the guidelines for group participation.
From *The Home-School Connection* by Jacqueline McGilp and Maureen Michael, Eleanor Curtain Publishing, 1994. This page may be reproduced for use in a school discussion program.

PARENTS AND SCHOOLS

☆ Parents and teachers share responsibility for children's learning.

☆ The school encourages parents to taken an active interest in their children's progress.

☆ Parents adopt many roles in schools.

☆ What is the school policy on parent participation?

☆ What supportive roles do parents exercise?
  • tuckshop
  • school board

☆ What educational roles do parents have?
  • correctors of writing
  • helpers with reading

☆ What proportion of the parents in our school would act as spectators, instructors or learners in our school?

☆ Which role appeals to you? Why?

ALL PARENTS ARE TEACHERS

☆ Parents teach their children:
- First words
- Personal hygiene
- Safety rules
- Values
- Social skills

☆ Parents teach by encouragement, demonstration, modelling, revising and monitoring children's efforts.

☆ What can you tell the school about the way your child learns?

☆ What proud memories do you have of teaching your child?

☆ What do schools expect parents to teach school-age children?

☆ In what do you find the school's expectations challenging and/or burdensome?

☆ Parents and teachers perform complementary roles in educating school-age children.

Figure 18, page 56, Discussion Starter 2
From *The Home-School Connection* by Jacqueline McGilp and Maureen Michael, Eleanor Curtain Publishing, 1994. This page may be reproduced for use in a school discussion program.

EDUCATION FOR LIVING

☆ Learning takes places everywhere that a child is.

☆ Education for Living involves the home, school and community.

☆ Parents and teachers reinforce the importance of gaining knowledge and skills for living.

☆ In what ways are you as parents presently educating your children for living?

☆ When are you initiators, facilitators, instructors or encouragers of learning for living? Give specific examples.

☆ What living skills would you like the school to develop now?

☆ Through what community experiences and excursions could the school extend children's learning?

☆ Make suggestions for an excursion in which children can practise a skill and learn a skill.

THE PENNYCOE PROJECT

☆ Parents can help provide a diverse and enriched curriculum for students.

☆ Personal contact influences parent participation.

☆ Parents are willing to be involved in schools in a concentrated way over a limited time.

☆ What kinds of occupational expertise could parents contribute to school learning programs?

☆ What hobbies, interests and ideas can you share with students?

☆ What value do you see in Pennycoe school initiatives?

☆ How does parental involvement at Pennycoe compare with parental activity at our school?

☆ What program can you initiate to involve parents?

Figure 20, page 56, Discussion Starter 4
From *The Home-School Connection* by Jacqueline McGilp and Maureen Michael, Eleanor Curtain Publishing, 1994. This page may be reproduced for use in a school discussion program.

EDUCATIONAL ROLES FOR PARENTS IN SCHOOLS

☆ Different roles have distinct characteristics.

☆ The roles of *spectator*, *learner* and *instructor* focus on children's learning.

☆ Parents and teachers combine roles when assisting students.

☆ What aspects of the case studies are familiar to our school?

☆ What school activities involve you as *learners*, *instructors* and *organisers*?

☆ What role would you like to develop? Why?

☆ Tell how you could adopt two of these three roles: *spectator*, *learner*, *instructor*.

HOME AND COMMUNITY SETTINGS

☆ School learning can be extended to the home and the community.

☆ Team work helps children's learning in every setting.

☆ What impressed you about each of the three case stories (The Hobson's run an Evening Class; Mr Hearne takes a Year 4 class; Parents organise an Art Excursion)?

☆ What opportunities did the case studies offer children?

☆ What difficulties do you foresee in offering similar parent sessions?

☆ Could our school plan for a few short parent sessions? Who would teach?

☆ Can we start with one level of the school? Which one? Why?

Figure 22, page 57, Discussion Starter 6
From *The Home-School Connection* by Jacqueline McGilp and Maureen Michael, Eleanor Curtain Publishing, 1994. This page may be reproduced for use in a school discussion program.

CREATING THE CLIMATE

☆ Parents and teachers affirm the contributions of each other to children's learning.

☆ In our school, when do parents tell the teachers about their children's progress and interests at home?

☆ In our school, when do teachers tell the parents about children's progress and interests at school?

☆ What encourages you to feel confident to share information about your child with the teachers? What encourages you to entrust that information to the teacher?

☆ The school is responsible for children's learning within the school program. Parental contribution to the school program is always at the school's invitation?

☆ How could you extend other parents' repertoires of roles so that the children benefit?

☆ Make suggestions of the contributions that you (or a small group of parents) could make to a specific class. Suggest the time and space needed.

Figure 23, page 57, Discussion Starter 7
From *The Home-School Connection* by Jacqueline McGilp and Maureen Michael, Eleanor Curtain Publishing, 1994. This page may be reproduced for use in a school discussion program.

TRAINING SESSIONS

☆ Training programs can equip parents for unfamiliar roles.

☆ Only a small number of parents presently contributes to learning activities at our school.

☆ Training sessions increase parent involvement.

☆ Parents and teachers are learners.

☆ What training is provided by the school for you?

☆ In what areas have you recently asked for help? Do other parents want this too?

☆ Which training formats appeal to you: lecture, workshop, observation, demonstration?

☆ Suggest some specific training sessions for a group of parents to enable them to help their children's learning.

☆ Work out a simple time frame for such training and practice over a one-month period.

CURRICULUM PLANNING SHEET

CURRICULUM:

Unit Focus / topic / concept:

Class:

Week

Goal

LEARNING EXPERIENCES

RESOURCES

PARENTAL CONTRIBUTION

EVALUATION

CHILDREN'S LEARNING

PARENTAL CONTRIBUTION

REFLECTION

Figure 25, page 58, A proforma for planning each curriculum segment
From *The Home-School Connection* by Jacqueline McGilp and Maureen Michael, Eleanor Curtain Publishing, 1994. This page may be reproduced for use in a school discussion program.

RECORD SHEET

Parent Contribution to Children's Learning

Date	Parent	Role (1-6)1	Task	Comment

1 Spectator; 2 Organiser; 3 Expert instructor; 4 Competent instructor; 5 Program-trained instructor; 6 Learner

Figure 26, page 58 , A proforma for monitoring parent participation
From *The Home-School Connection* by Jacqueline McGilp and Maureen Michael, Eleanor Curtain Publishing, 1994. This page may be reproduced for use in a school discussion program.

References

Bernstein, B. 1981, Social class and linguistic development : a theory of social learning. In *Education, economy and society* New York: The Free Press.

Braggett, E.J. 1980, *Parental involvement in children's education* Newcastle, NSW: University of NSW.

Gordon, I.J. 1970, Florida parent education early intervention projects: A longitudinal study. Illinois: ERIC Clearinghouse on Early Childhood Education Urban III, Florida University, Gainsville.

Gordon, I.J. 1979, The effects of parent involvement in schools. In R.S.Brandt *Partners, parents and schools* Virginia: Association for Supervision and Curriculum Development.

McConnell, B. 1979, Individualised bilingual instructions. Final evaluation, 1977-78 Program Year. No 13 in the series. Washington DC: Report to the US Office of Education, Division of Bilingual Education.

McGilp, E.J. 1991, *Parents teaching in schools*. Set I May. New Zealand Council for Educational Research and Australian Council for Educational Research.

McGilp, E.J. 1992, School community based on home-school relations. In *Of Visions and Directions* Vol, 5, No 2, June 1992.

McGilp, E.J. 1993 Parental involvement in children's artistic learning. In F. Smit, W. Van Esch, J.Walberg (eds). *Parental involvement in schools*. Nijmegen: Institute of Applied Social Science.

Pettit, D. 1980, *Opening up schools: school and community in Australia* Ringwood: Penguin Books.

Schikedanz, J.A. 1977, Parents, teachers and early education. In B. Persky and L. Colubcheck (eds) *Early Childhood* Wayne, New Jersey: Avery Publishing.

Toomey, D.M. 1980, How parent participation in schools can add to educational inequality. Bundoora: La Trobe University. (Unpublished paper)

Additional Reading:

Leler, H. 1983, Parent education and involvement in relation to the school and to parents of school-aged children. In *Parents, education and public policy* Norwood, New Jersey: Ablex Publishing.

Tizard, B., and Hughes, M. 1984, *Young children learning: talking and thinking at home and at school* London: Fontana Paperbacks.

Topping, K. 1986, *Parents as educators* London: Croom Helm.

Index

Benefits 19, 40
  parental involvement in children's learning 19, 20-24
  social contact 19
  change in attitude 19

Case Stories 25
  Hobsons run an evening session 26-30
  Hearne takes a year 4 class 30-32
  Parents organise an art excursion 31-36
  Jim Read 24
  Mary McNab 23
  Joy Hass 21
  Joy Adams 22
  Sue Mills 20
  Bob Smith 23
Children's Poetry 27, 33, 34, 35, 36
Children's Work 18, 24, 29, 30, 33, 34, 35, 36
Creating the Climate 39, 40, 41
  building a successful repertoire 40-43
Community Involvement in Education 2, 5, 9, 10
Curriculum 18
Curriculum Plan 58
Curriculum Analysis Sheet 58

Discussion Program 49
  advantages of discussion program 50
  outcomes of discussion program 49
  the program 49
  program goals 51, 53, 54
  content and sequence 53
  roles and responsibilities 54
  organisation 50-51
  monitoring the program 55
  presentation 51
  introductory session 51-52
  size of groups 51, 54
  duration of session 54
  group guidelines 54, 55
  review sheet 51
Difficulties
  criticism 41
  favouritism 41
  fear 41
  interference 41
  isolation 41
  stress 41
Discussion Starters
  for the School Community 54, 55
  for teachers 54, 55, 57

Education for Living
  art excursion 9, 10, 31, 32
  at the factory 9
  at the retirement hostel 9
  at sports events 9
  at the supermarket 8

Home-School Learning Connection 2, 3, 41
Home and Community Settings 25-39
  Hobsons run an evening session 26-30
  Hearne takes a Year 4 class 30
  Parents organise an art excursion 31-36
  guidelines 34-39

Management 43
  time 43
  space 43

Parents Affirm School Learning 40
Parents Teach 5, 6
   parents reinforce school learning
      6, 40, 50
   skills development in the home 49
   ways in which parents teach 5, 6, 7
   parents are proud teachers 7
   children in families 7
Parents' Guide 32, 36
Pennycoe Primary School 4, 13-17, 48

Questionnaire 14, 15

Roles For Parents
   audience 2
   decisionmakers 2
   encouragers 11
   evaluators 11
   facilitators 10
   fundraisers 2
   initiators 10
   learners 23
   organisers 3, 19, 21, 23, 24
   policymakers 2, 23
   spectators 2, 20, 23, 24
   instructors, 3, 10, 11, 21, 22, 23, 24, 25
   instructors, expert 3, 21
   instructors, competent 3, 22
   instructors, skilled if trained 3, 22

School's Responsibility 42, 45

Training Modes 46
   demonstration 47
   lecture 46
   workshops 46
   observation 47
   timing of sessions 47

Training Sessions 44
   results of training session 46
   responsibility 45
   who does the training 45

Other titles by Australian authors

Thinking for Themselves

Developing strategies for reflective learning

Jent Wilson and Lesley Wing Jan

By encouraging children to think about their learning and to become aware of and control their thinking processes, teachers can help them to become active, responsible learners – learners who can make their own decisions, choose appropriate strategies, assess their own work and set their own goals. *Thinking for Themselves* provides activities for the development of skills and strategies within a range of existing programs and starting points and ideas to help the implementation of reflective teaching and learning programs.

Contents: Getting started *Developing the appropriate learning environment *Program planning *Negotiating with students *Questioning and self-assessment techniques.

ISBN 0 435 08805 X illustrated 124pp

I Teach

A guide to inspiring classroom leadership

Joan Dalton and Julie Boyd

Specific and practical insights into the 'what' and 'how' of effective learning and teaching presented succinctly and visually.

Contents: Identify your goals *Walk the leader's walk *Build relationships with others *Create a community of learners *Empower growth in others *Work on self-growth – identify personal strengths, highlight areas for self-improvement and plan for balanced leadership.

ISBN 0 435 08782 7 illustrated 128pp

The Big Picture

Integrating students' learning

Edited by Marilyn Woolley and Keith Pigdon

The Big Picture addresses the key issues which are central to the idea of the integrated curriculum and translates them into practical classroom advice.

Contents: Context and framework: the ideas which drive teachers' curriculum planning *A planning model: bringing the components together in an organised yet flexible structure *The model in practice: activities and strategies *Language and the integrated curriculum: integrated learning and specific curriculum practice *Assessment and evaluation: for the learner, the teacher and the community *Whole school change: it starts in your classroom.

ISBN 0 435 08792 4 illustrated 128pp

One Teacher's Classroom

Strategies for successful teaching and learning

Dale Gordon

Within the context the whole language learning, this is record of the successful strategies of an experienced, competent and dedicated teacher who has built up a framework of teaching practice. The book provides models, guidelines and strategies to support these aims.

Contents: Creating a learning environment: providing time, providing a place, providing resources *Making learning easier for learners: integrating the conditions for learning, providing real reasons to learn, demonstrating learning *Allowing learners to function at their full potential: taking responsibility, approximation, expectations for learning *Finding out about learning: feedback, assessment and reporting.

ISBN 1 875327 15 0 illustrated 128pp

Becoming Responsible Learners

Strategies for positive classroom management

Joan Dalton and Mark Collis

An extremely practical and highly readable book on strategies and guide-lines for classroom management, this best-selling book is the result of observing effective collaborative teachers at work and talking to them about their beliefs and classroom practices. *Becoming Responsible Learners* is an invaluable asset to teachers who want to encourage children to take responsibility for their own learning and behaviour.

ISBN 0 435 08568 9 illustrated 80pp

The Collaborative Classroom

A guide to co-operative learning

Susan and Tim Hill

The Collaborative Classroom is a creative and practical guide for teachers who want to implement and gain maximum benefit for students from co-operative learning. The book focuses and identifies the areas where co-operative skills are needed: forming groups and managing differences. *The Collaborative Classroom* is both practical and encouraging and includes dozens of activities to get the beginning teacher started.

ISBN 0 435 08525 5 illustrated 162pp

The Literacy Agenda

Issues for the nineties

Elaine Furniss and Pamela Green, Editors

A book to provoke, encourage and inspire you to 'have a go' at confronting the key issues of literacy development in your own classroom. Each chapter is a collaboration between a leading teacher educator and a classroom teacher, so that the practical implications of the issues are always addressed.

Contents: How children learn to read *What happens if they don't succeed *Equal opportunities for girls and boys *How to use the literacy cultures that children bring to the classroom *The sort of talk that takes place in classrooms *Assessment procedures *Second language learners *How to involve parents.

ISBN 0 435 08707 X illustrated 178pp

Literacy Evaluation

Issues and practicalities

Christine Bouffler, Editor

The increasing pressure for greater accountability has put assessment high on the educational agenda. There are four major groups requiring performance information: students, teachers, parents and educational systems. *Literacy Evaluation* surveys some of the recent developments in language assessment – in the United States, the United Kingdom and in Australia – which attempt to satisfy the needs of these groups.

ISBN 0 345 08791 6 120pp

Teach On

Teaching strategies for reading and writing workshops

David Hornsby, Jo-Ann Parry and Deborah Sukarno

Teach On recognises the importance of two things: first, that for effective learning to occur, teachers must 'tune in' to children's strengths and needs; second, that they must teach! This practical book outlines several strategies and procedures that have been successful in classrooms where whole language philosophy guides the teacher's program.

ISBN 0 453 08790 8 84pp

Each of these titles is published by Heinemann